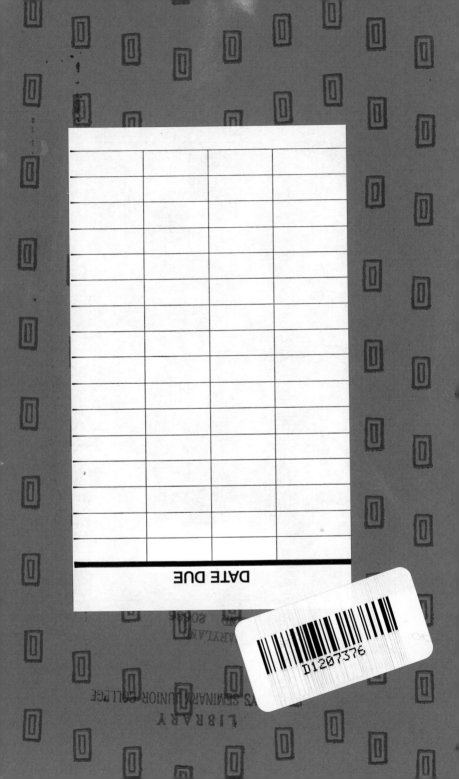

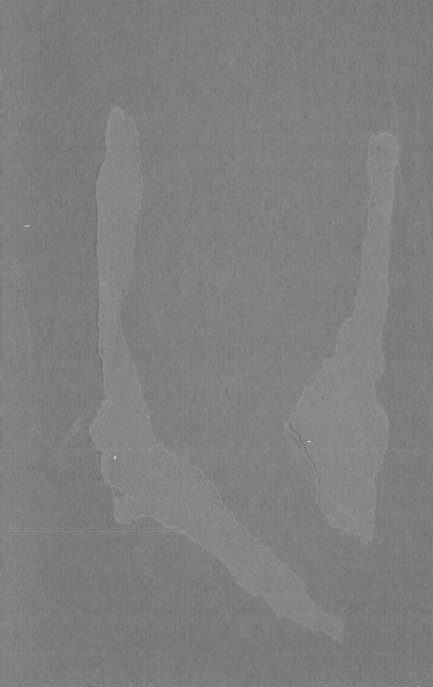

11833

**Whaling Ship
drawn by Manjiro**

MANJIRO, THE MAN WHO
DISCOVERED AMERICA

Cast thy bread upon the waters:
for thou shalt find it after many days.
Ecclesiastes 11:1

MANJIRO,
THE MAN
WHO
DISCOVERED
AMERICA

BY

HISAKAZU KANEKO

HOUGHTON MIFFLIN COMPANY BOSTON

The Riverside Press Cambridge

PREFACE

THIS IS a story of Manjiro Nakahama alias John Mung, a fisherman's boy who was shipwrecked and rescued by the *John Howland*, a New Bedford whaling ship, from an uncharted island in the Pacific in 1841 when, incidentally, Herman Melville, author of *Moby Dick*, was sailing in another New Bedford whaling ship, the *Acushnet*, in the same waters. Under the fatherly care of the captain of the whaling ship, Manjiro was taken to America as the first Japanese to be educated and to live there, and later he managed to return to his native land, then pursuing a rigorous isolation policy which prohibited anyone from entering the country on pain of death. He became a "voice in the wilderness" and helped open his countrymen's eyes to modern civilization, playing no small part in aiding his country's gradual evolution from feudalism to democracy. More than a century has elapsed since then, but the spirit of adventure and progress and the virtues of kindness and goodwill as exemplified in his life are alive today.

It may be opportune to publish a book of this kind at this particular time when we have just celebrated the centennial of Commodore Perry's expedition to Japan, for it was none other than Commodore Perry who drastically changed the course of Manjiro's life and gave him the opportunity to turn his ability and experience to the best account for his country at its crisis. This book is an attempt to present as clearly as possible, and in some detail, the life and adventure of Manjiro and the milieu in which he lived, so that the reader may enjoy this delightful episode in the history of Japanese-American relations.

I have been able to get access to several records and documents attributed to the officials who investigated Manjiro and the other shipwrecked men concerning their experiences abroad, which I have freely used as source material for my book. I am also greatly indebted to the two Japanese books, Mr. Masuji Ibuse's *The Shipwreck Story of John Manjiro* and *A Biography of Manjiro Nakahama* written by his son, Dr. Toichiro Nakahama. Also I want to record my indebtedness to "The Presentation of a Samurai Sword to the Town of Fairhaven" and "Fairhaven, Massachusetts" which the Millicent Library of Fairhaven, Mass., kindly sent me. My thanks for sympathy and encouragement are many, and are due to Mr. Philip F. Purrington, Curator of the Old Dartmouth Historical Society and the Whaling Museum, New Bedford, Mass., who unstintedly furnished me with much of the hitherto unknown Fairhaven information about Manjiro; to Mrs. P. W. E.,

Mr. W. C. B., and many others who have taken the trouble to read the manuscript or the proof and who have given me much valuable suggestion and advice, without which this book would not have been materialized.

HISAKAZU KANEKO

CONTENTS

Whaling Ship
drawn by Manjiro

MANJIRO, THE MAN WHO
DISCOVERED AMERICA

A
SHIPWRECK

Manjiro was born in the tenth year of the Bunsei Era (1827) in a lonely fishing village called Nakanohama, in the Province of Tosa where the warm Black Current of the Pacific Ocean ceaselessly washes its craggy coast. His father Etsuke died when Manjiro was only nine years old and his widowed mother, Shio, with her lean hands had to feed her five ever hungry children. So poor was she that she could not afford to send the children to a nearby Buddhist temple for a simple education. Manjiro had to work. When he was thirteen years old, he put to sea in a fishing boat and unhooked fish from the lines to get what little money he could earn and help his widowed mother eke out a scanty livelihood.

On the morning of the fifth of January, 1841, when he

was fourteen years old, he took to the sea, bright and early, from Usaura with Denzo, aged thirty-eight, Jusuke, aged twenty-five, and Goemon, aged fifteen, both brothers of Denzo, and Toraemon, aged twenty-six, in an attempt to catch the sea bass that would come riding along in the tide of the New Year. The boat, which belonged to one Toku-nojo of Usaura, was loaded with three bushels of rice and quantities of other food, firewood and fresh water so that they could engage in fishing for several days on end.

That day, when the boat reached a point about twenty-eight miles away from Usaura, they cast all the nets they had, but there was not a fish to be caught. In the evening they steered the boat behind the Cape of Yaso to take shelter from the wind and waited for the light of day. The next morning they went out thirty miles off the coast of Ashizuri to try their luck with rods and lines, but they were as luckless as the day before. So they gave up fishing for the day and again rowed back near the shore to stay for the night.

On the seventh day they rowed out again about thirty miles from the Cape of Ashizuri, but the catch was as poor as ever. Then, suddenly, a strong monkey-and-cock wind began to blow, so they decided to make for land before they were overtaken by a storm. When the boat had traversed about ten miles of the intervening sea it ran into such a large shoal of mackerel and sea bream that the sea seemed to have taken on a dark purplish color. Denzo spurred the others into action and cast six bucketfuls of nets. In the meantime the sky grew dark and the wind blew full blast, threatening to overturn the boat at any moment. Terrified out of their wits, they tried to haul in the nets but as the billows swelled mountain-high, tossing the boat about, they barely managed to recover three bucket-fuls of nets and rowed for their lives toward the shore.

Soon the rain began to fall and a splashy mist rose from the sea until it became so thick that nothing was to be seen an inch ahead. They rowed as hard as they could, but soon they became too exhausted to prevent the boat from being carried away by the wind and waves like a fallen leaf in a rapid stream. Soon night fell. Their clothes were drenched with salty water and the cold pierced their bodies. They had only one oar left now and the rudder and the canvases were also carried away by the waves. There was nothing they could do. They only knelt down on the planks and prayed to the gods and to Buddha, and asked for their divine protection. The boat seemed to be drifting south-ward. The wind still raged and there was no prospect of fine weather next morning.

It was said that a storm that had not blown over by the dawn was sure to blow just as hard all next day. Fortunately, the boat itself remained undamaged and drifted on. Soon they saw in the distance, be-tween the peaks of swelling billows and through the murky rain, Cape Muroto and its straggling houses. On one of the hills of this cape there was a watchman's lodge called "Mountain View" where villagers kept a lookout for whales. Had the watchmen there seen the boat in distress, they would surely have put out a ship to come to their rescue. All the men in the rudderless boat, madly waving their hands and scratching their heads in grief, shouted at the top of their lungs, "Help! Help!" But as swift as thought, the boat was carried away while Cape Muroto receded into the distance. A little after noon, what seemed to be the mountain range of Kishu came into sight above the rain-brewing cloud but in a few moments it, too, dis-appeared in the mist and rain. The last oar was gone with the waves, and with it the hope of turning back the boat, which was now no better than a body without limbs. At night the cold wind blew so hard that their drenched clothes were frozen and small icicles settled on their sleeves and the knots of their sashes. They barely prevented themselves from being frozen to death by burning some planks and straw mats to keep warm. Their rice was all gone now, and they had to catch fish to survive.

On the tenth day a drizzling rain was falling. The cold seemed to be particularly penetrating that day and much worse than the cold of the night. Small icicles hung not only from their sleeves and sashes but also from the shaggy hair of Denzo. The sleet, blown into his topknot, melted and dripped down his spine. As the drinking water was all gone, they scraped sleet together and drank it, and ate the icicles gathered from their sleeves. Goemon's hands and feet were numb with cold so he shudderingly pulled a straw mat over himself and breathed faintly.

On the eleventh day the wind and rain grew harder than ever. Denzo and Toraemon made a roof out of the re-maining canvases and split the planks and burned them in order to make sick Goemon warm and comfortable as best they could. He was suffering from a cold with fever, hunger and exhaustion. Denzo produced from a pouch a talisman, a small piece of paper on which something was written, and put it into the mouth of Goemon as if it were a medicine. Soon Goemon's fever seemed to have abated considerably.

By the twelfth day the rain seemed a little weakened and it was not so severely cold any more. While looking out toward the distant sea about noon, they sighted a flock of white birds called Tokuro by the fishermen of Tosa, which were believed to be the sign of an island nearby. Denzo, pointing toward the birds, told the fever-stricken Goemon to look at the Tokuro. Whereupon Goemon half rose and opened his eyes narrowly to see the distant sky where they were flying. Then as soon as he lay flat again, he began to cry aloud, for he was a fainthearted boy although he was born in the year of the wild boar.

The flock of white birds was winging its way gracefully toward the southeastern horizon and soon disappeared in the rain-swollen clouds. Denzo, Jusuke, Toraemon and Manjiro peered over the sea under the dark cloud and kept a hard lookout. As they expected, toward the evening they sighted an island in the direction in which the white birds had disappeared.

Overjoyed at the sight of the island, they pulled themselves together and erected a remaining sail yard and spread a jib over it. Denzo steered the boat with a plank, as best he could. Toraemon and Jusuke worked at the sail yard and the jib and Manjiro ladled out the bilge water so that the boat headed for the island slowly but safely.

By the time they reached the island it was almost dark. Moreover, like so many other uncharted islands, the shore of this island was fringed with a steep cliff and the billows were madly dashing and breaking against it. Reefs were everywhere to defy their approach and no place was to be found where they could steer in or cast anchor safely. To discover what they could, they went around the island only to find that everywhere the rugged cliff rose high against the sky and there was no beach on which to land.

Late at night the rain stopped at last and a pale blue

moon loomed out in the rain-washed sky. In its faint light they saw sea bass swarming by the rocks, so they produced a fishing tackle and angled for them before they did anything else. They were so hungry that they ate with great gusto the live fish just as they were taken out of the sea. When this primitive feast was over they felt somewhat refreshed, but they decided not to risk their lives by making a desperate attempt at landing on this uncharted island in the faint light of the moon when the sea was still choppy. So they kept the boat away from the island as far as the anchor rope permitted and cast anchor "to sleep in the cradle of the deep" with the dark mass of cliff in full view.

The next morning — the thirteenth — Goemon became better but the others had not completely recovered from exhaustion and exposure. They felt as if all their strength had gone and when they pulled at the rope to weigh anchor, their knees gave way and they felt all the more hungry and exhausted. As if it were stuck to the bottom of the sea, the anchor refused to come up, no matter how hard they pulled at the anchor rope. So they put their heads together. "There's no hope of life, if we stay in this rudderless boat," said Denzo. "If it were only possible to get on that island, we might be able to save our lives by some good fortune. But I want to point out," he continued, "that any attempt at going to that cliff in this broken boat will surely be the death of us all."

While everyone thought hard, Toraemon put in, "Death stares us in the face. We shall be lucky if we are alive tomorrow. Since that is the case, why not push this boat along the cliff and jump to the island, sink or swim?" Jusuke seconded it and they all agreed. Denzo at once made a makeshift rudder by putting planks together and said he would hold it with Jusuke. Toraemon, Manjiro and Goemon decided to pull the oars made of planks and use a roof beam as a substitute for a boating pole. Thus they were ready to stake their lives in the face of this obvious risk.

Denzo cut off the anchor rope with a hatchet. The boat rolled and shook violently as it dashed off toward the cliff. Steered through the dangerous rocks, it was brought near the entrance of an opening in the cliff when suddenly it was heaved up on the top of a billow and knocked against a corner of the rugged cliff. Toraemon and Goemon lost no time in leaping onto the corner of the cliff and clambered up its side by putting their feet in what small crevices they could find. The other three men were about to follow the example of Toraemon and Goemon now climbing the cliff when another billow came dashing on, tossing the boat high on its peak. Instantly, the boat careened and then overturned and was caught between the two rocks. Manjiro was thrown into the waves, which in a moment dragged him into their depths, but he finally managed to come to the surface and swim across to the cliff. Denzo and Jusuke were also whirled into the sea, together with the makeshift rudder, down to the bottom of the opening in the cliff, and there they struggled in vain under the boat for a moment. But the oncoming swell extricated the entrapped boat from between the rocks and bore it away as it receded toward the open sea, while both Denzo and Jusuke were hurled upon the rock in the seething white foam. Thus they narrowly escaped from the jaws of death and they too clambered up the cliff to safety.

Jusuke must have knocked one of his feet violently against the rock and injured it when he was hurled upon the cliff, for no sooner had he reached the top of the cliff than his strength gave way and he fell flat on his face. The boat was smashed to bits against the cliff when it came back riding on another billow and its remains were soon swallowed up in the churning and eddying sea.

ON
AN ISLAND
OF
ALBATROSS

THE ISLAND, about two miles in circumference, stood thick with crags rising skyward and not a living soul was to be found there. The only vegetation was a kind of dwarfish reed. When Manjiro saw the island, he at once recalled the picture of the Mountains of Swords in Hell which the village priest had shown his family on a certain Buddhist festival day. At once, all went out in quest of a spring in the deep recesses among the rocks. They discovered a cave about twelve feet square in a rocky hill where a little water was trickling through a crevice. Seashells were scattered about the entrance to testify that men had once lived here. They cleaned the place at once as best they could and decided to make it their temporary shelter. Again they went in search of more water and at last one of them discovered a place where rain water had collected in a fairly large hollow of a rock. They put their lips to this well and quenched their thirst. The little pool of water was the only place where they could get drinking water. There was nothing edible to be found on the island except the albatrosses which were flying over the island or flocking together on the rocks.

That night they tried to sleep in the cave, but the cold wind blew in so hard that they were unable to do so. Taking advantage of the moonlight, they went down to the shore and picked up some of the washed-up planks and canvas and carried them back to the cave. They improvised a door in order to prevent the cold wind from blowing into the cave. Then they snuggled close to one another to keep warm and tried to sleep, but now they felt very lonely. So they kept on talking to one another in an attempt to forget their unbearable restlessness.

"What do you think," asked Denzo, "is the name of this island? It seems far out in the south. But it cannot be one of those southern islands — it is too cold for that. Perhaps, we are in the extreme east." The question which was beyond the comprehension of an experienced fisherman like Denzo naturally remained a mystery to the rest of them.

"Is this a part of Japan?" put in Toraemon. "If the island is in the extreme east, it must be somewhere further east than Izu. But I have never in my life heard that if you go further east it gets colder. Doesn't the end of the earth lie in the north?"

"As for the end of the earth," explained Denzo, "it makes no difference which way you go, east or west or south or north. It is a fact that the end of the earth lies evenly in the east, west, south and north. I don't know whether or not this island lies at the end of the earth, but I do know that a rescue ship will not come this way tomorrow or the day after tomorrow, for that matter. It may be that we must live on this rocky island for many years to come. But I have a good idea and there is no harm in practicing it, as far as I can see. Why not imagine this is the beginning of a new world and start a life all over again? Let everyone be big and bold in heart."

The four men, seeing no objection to this proposition, agreed to it unanimously. In other words, they decided to call that memorable day the beginning of the First Year of the Era of the Solitary Island and band together to make life on the island as much worth living as possible and disavow all the sceptical philosophies of life.

The next day, January 14, as soon as they awoke, they went out of the cave in search of food. The sea still looked too rough for them to catch fish and shellfish and so instead they decided to capture albatrosses which flew down to the island in such large numbers. The birds looked like snow covering the craggy tops of the island. They were so tame and unafraid of the stalking men that they were easily caught one after another. Having caught almost too many to carry, the men returned to the cave with a heavy load of the birds. With the nails they had taken out of the planks, they prepared the meat and feasted on it, although they found that the bird meat was not half so tasty as fish or clams. They pounded the leftover bird meat with a stone and dried it in the sun, calling it stone-baked, and sometimes they preserved the meat in salt for a change of taste.

Denzo came back with the three small pails that also

had been pushed up on the shore by the waves. After fixing them in such a way that the rain water would drip into them, he designated them as "wells." The one which looked the newest of the three was called "the Well of Life"; the one shaped like a measure box branded with a character "Yamaju" on it was called "the Well of Reserve"; and one which was like a barrel of *shoyu* sauce was called "the Well of Spring Water." And he prescribed a strict law concerning the use of the "wells" — that the water in these pails after a rainfall should not be drunk as long as the water in the hollow of the rock stayed. The reason was that the water of the rock hollow would soon be dried up by the sun.

The thing that inconvenienced them most was the fact that they could not drink water as much as they wished. When they had been there about a month, it happened that a spell of dry weather settled down for about twenty days without any prospect of rain. Needless to say, the water in the hollow of the rock was completely gone. The water in "the Well of Spring Water" and in "the Well of Reserve" was gone and even the last pailful of water in "the Well of Life" too was used up. They gave a feeling of moisture to their mouths by chewing stems of a grass which contained some juice. Sometimes they licked at the rock wet with the night's dew. After this bitter experience Denzo prescribed three regulations concerning the use of the water which were much more strict:

Article I. Don't waste the water. The unlawful act of drinking on the sly is strictly forbidden.

Article II. For each albatross to be eaten, water in one oyster shell is allowed. Refrain by all means from drinking more than this allotment.

Article III. Don't drink water when you eat seaweed,

etc. Try to wipe off the salt as best you can from the sea-weed before you eat it. It is advisable in this connection to swallow spittle in the mouth.

These were the regulations, but as the men were all un-lettered, they learned the regulations by heart and kept them faithfully.

They were so emaciated and so pitiable to look at that any metaphor would be too dull to describe them. Their food was limited to albatross, seaweed and shellfish, which had to be eaten raw since the flint, pots, kettles and other cooking utensils had been all lost when the boat capsized. Denzo made something like cotton out of a handful of blades of withered reed by threshing them thoroughly. Again and again he struck this cottonlike material together with a nail between two stones, hoping to produce fire, but no matter how hard he tried, it was all in vain.

The albatrosses which once were so tame were beginning to fear the men. When the hunters approached to within a few yards, the birds would run off and finally fly away if the men continued to chase them. So, lying in ambush behind a rock, they would jump upon the birds when they came near enough and club them or stone them. This made the birds all the more wary and at last they took refuge up in the high rocky mountains. It was only among the steep rocks which the men could not reach that the birds laid their eggs and hatched their broods. Then at the end of May, they began their migration to an unknown distant place together with their fledglings.

About this time Denzo had an accident which caused him a serious wound. He had been chasing birds all day on a rocky fell that rose above the cave. He finally man-aged to catch two and threw them down from the top of the cliff toward the cave entrance. As he was clambering down, he suddenly lost his footing and fell down the precipice. The fall might have killed him had it not been broken by a clump of reeds to which he managed to cling. Although he was bruised all over his body, he managed to get back to the cave. After this accident Denzo gradually became weaker — so weak in fact that he lingered inside the cave day in and day out.

Jusuke, younger brother of Denzo, finding his wounded leg getting no better, began also to stay in the cave to be nursed by Denzo. Toraemon and Goemon, though not really ill, looked feebler and thinner and were in a constant state of depression.

Manjiro alone remained strong both in body and spirit. One day, he went on a brave adventure — scaling the highest eminence on the island, which, although it was an ascent of only a quarter of a mile, had remained unchallenged, so steep and perilous was it. He reached the top after a hard climb over the steep side of the fell. There he found a spacious flat place and what appeared to be an old well, the sides of which were lined with stones, with a small pool of dark water at the weed-covered bottom. Not far from this old well there were what appeared to be two tombstones, somewhat oblong in shape, but they were so weather-beaten that the characters on them were almost completely obliterated. While Manjiro stood there looking around blankly for some time, he suddenly noticed more than ten whales floating peacefully out in the sea.

Upon returning to the cave, he told Denzo and the others how he had seen what appeared to be an old well and two tombstones on the top of the fell. Denzo asked whether the tombs were covered with moss, and he seemed to be thinking of his old home in Nishinohama where his ancestral tombs were. Suddenly he covered his face with his hands and said, "Must we die like the men who lie under those tombstones?" Jusuke, Toraemon and Goemon all began to cry. After a while Denzo ceased to weep, but when Manjiro began to tell how he had sighted a school of whales, Denzo wept all over again and said, "My dear Manjiro, it is a sin to tell such a thing." For he was overcome at that moment with an irresistible desire to eat a big juicy steak of whale meat.

It was on June 27 that a piece of good fortune unexpectedly came their way. That morning Manjiro had gone down to the seaside bright and early and was picking up some shellfish when he happened to sight a tiny black dot far away on the horizon. "It's a ship!" He danced with joy and his voice rang in the quiet morning of the lonely island. "Hurray! It's a ship! Goemon Nushi! Toraemon Nushi! A ship is sighted!" They had also come to the water's edge to pick up some shellfish. Running up to where he was, they looked out over the sea and they too jumped for joy. It was a ship, to be sure! Moreover, it seemed to be coming toward the island. It was a strange ship of a strange country with many sails spreading on its three masts. Now it came so near that men in "pipelike sleeves" could be seen clearly walking on the deck. All of a sudden, however, she changed her course toward the northwest and was ready to sail away apparently in utter disregard of the island and the stranded men on it.

"Oh, Buddha! Hear our prayer and don't let that ship go away!" said Goemon, kneeling on the beach. But the ship continued its course and sailed away from the island. Toraemon was so disappointed that, accompanied by Goemon, he went back to the entrance of the cave where he lay and cried bitterly. Manjiro tried to gather shellfish and seaweed at the beach since he was hungry and Jusuke had eaten almost nothing for the last two or three days. But he could do nothing of the sort. He simply stood on the beach watching the receding ship and prayed that it would come back to the island by some miracle. Suddenly he noticed the ship in the offing drop anchor and put out two boats. They were coming to the island too! Manjiro ran. He ran to the entrance of the cave where Toraemon and Goemon were. He shouted, "The boats! They are coming! Look!" The three men ran up a small hill nearby and repeatedly shouted to inform the boats that there were shipwrecked men on the island and that they must come to the island at once. The men picked up a plank that had been thrown up on the shore by the waves and tying Toraemon's checkered underwear to one end of it, they waved it furiously until they almost fainted. The boats apparently understood what it was all about, for they veered their course and came straight toward the stranded men.

The men on the island waved their hands as much as to say, "Come quick, come quick!" and the men in the boats took off their caps in response. They came quite close to the shore now, but finding no place to land, the strangers in the boats made signs to them to take off their clothes and tie them on their heads and swim across. But the three men on the cliff hesitated for some time, a little afraid of those red-haired and blue-eyed foreigners with white skin. They noticed that there was a black man too. Manjiro, determined and courageous, went down the cliff and taking off his clothes, tied them on his head and jumped into the sea just as the strangers had instructed him. They rowed up one of the boats and helped him into it. Thinking it was God's help, Manjiro knelt down and worshiped the strangers in gratitude. At this the black sailor burst out laughing. Goemon and then Toraemon jumped into the sea, each carrying his kimono on his head to be rescued in the same way.

But those three men were in such an excitement that they forgot all about Denzo and Jusuke, who were lying weak and feeble back in the cave. Toraemon tried to make the strangers understand how the matter stood, but his words being of no use, he pointed to the island and made signs that there were still two men left there. Then one of the white sailors said something to the others and they rowed back to the shore right under the cave. At this moment Denzo was wrapping a piece of cloth around one of Jusuke's feet. Suddenly a black man came into the cave uttering an outlandish language and tried to drag Denzo out. Denzo's heart leapt into his mouth and he tried to run away from the black man, when a white man appeared and stood between the two making signs as much as to say, "Calm down! Calm down! We are not going to eat you. Your friends have already been rescued in our boat. We are all friends."

The strange white man smiled good-naturedly, while the strange black man grinned showing terribly white teeth. Denzo heaved a sigh of relief and exchanging glances with Jusuke said, "Let's go." Then he went down the cliff, helped by the white man while Jusuke followed almost carried in the arms of the black man. Sure enough, Goemon, Toraemon and Manjiro were already standing in the boat, meek and smiling.

Denzo took off his kimono and tying it on his head, he

threw himself into the sea as suggested by the white man. The black man, carrying Jusuke in his arm, caught at a rope which had been tossed from the boat and both were pulled up safely.

The white man made signs to Denzo as much as to say, "You have not forgotten any valuable things in the cave, have you? If you have, don't hesitate to say so, for we shall send for them."

"Sir, we are only poor stranded men," Denzo managed to answer also by a gesture, "how is it possible that we should have left some valuable things on the island? Indeed, our eyes are filled with tears of thankfulness for all you have done to save us from the island."

"We are very happy, too," said the white man. "But let us hear what you have left in the cave. Speak up."

"Kimono, bird feathers, the shells of turtles, and the dried meat of birds."

The white man nodded a great nod and told the black man something in a strange tongue. They began to pull the oars smoothly toward the ship out in the sea, three times faster than an ordinary five-oared Japanese boat. The setting sun was already hovering over the horizon when the two boats reached the waiting ship.

On this day Captain Whitfield of the *John Howland* made the following simple entry in his logbook:

Sunday, June 27, 1841.

This day light winds from the S.E. The Isle in sight 26 1.00 p.m. Sent in two boats to see if there were any turtles. Found 5 poor distressed people on the Isle. Took them off. Could not understand anything from them more than that they were hungry. Made the latitude of the Isle 30 deg. 31 min. N.

ON A
RESCUE
SHIP

THE SHIP which rescued the five Japanese fishermen was a large vessel with three tall masts hoisting more than ten sails and jibs and spreading its weblike cordage in all directions. The main truck perching high on the royal topmast was faintly visible through the cloud of shrouds, yards and sails, and it seemed to reach the sky. A long jib boom was sticking far out over the water from the bow like an arm of a giant. The crew consisted of more than thirty men both white and black. *John Howland* was the name of the ship; it was a whaler from New Bedford, Massachusetts, U.S.A., and the captain was Mr. William H. Whitfield.

The rescued men, either half naked or in tattered kimono, were ghostly emaciated and sick from long hunger and exposure, with their lifeless faces half hidden in their long, dry, shaggy hair. When they were brought before Captain Whitfield for questioning, some of them were unable to stand and weakly squatted on the deck. They all looked at the captain feebly from the bottom of their deeply sunken eyes, half in fear, half in expectation. "You have saved us and you can do anything you like to us," they seemed to say.

The captain smiled a little and asked several questions, "Where do you come from?" or "What have you been doing on that island?" and so on. They simply shook their heads or waved their hands to show that they could not understand what he was talking about. They said timidly something in their own tongue, but he could not make out a word. All he could gather from their gestures was that they were very, very hungry.

Then the captain sent for the chief cook and told him, "Give them some food at once, but remember, don't give them too much before they have fully recovered."

A little later, the captain somehow was able to find out that they were shipwrecked Japanese fishermen who had been stranded on the island for six months.

The next morning, June 28, the captain ordered that several men together with Manjiro be sent in a boat to the cave of the island to bring back the belongings that the shipwrecked men might have left on the island. Manjiro could not understand why he alone was to be taken to the island with those men. He feared they might be taking him to the island to leave him there because he was too young to be a sailor. So he cried and begged in his own language, "Let me stay on the ship with my countrymen, for Heaven's sake." But it was no use. It was with great difficulty, however, that he understood at last that he was only going to the island to be their guide. After searching the cave thoroughly, they brought back what they found to the ship — old clothes, feathers, and turtle shells. The five men thanked the captain from the bottom of their hearts for his kindness but those moldy clothes and smelly feathers seemed no longer of any use to them now.

The captain made the following entry in the logbook of the *John Howland* on that day:

Monday, June 28, 1841
This day light winds from S. E. the island in sight. To the Westward, stood to the S. W. at 1 P. M. landed and brought off what few clothes the five men left.

They were given coats and leather boots and although they did not feel so uncomfortable in the close-fitting coats which were quite different from their kimonos, they found that the leather boots were almost unbearable.

A little before noon that day, the ship weighed anchor and headed southeast. The five men were shown into a room below, which appeared as wide as an eight-mat room, and were told they had better take a good rest there. Three days later they recovered their spirits and in five days their bodies regained their former strength. They did not like to be idling away their time, so on the seventh day they said to the captain that they were willing to do some work along with the crew men.

Jusuke's injured foot was gradually getting better under the care of the first officer. He applied an acid-smelling plaster to the affected part, covering it with a piece of oiled paper, and then he bandaged it. As it was improving day by day, Denzo and Toraemon were much impressed by the skillful treatment which the American seaman had administered.

On the eighth day the ship took its course toward the

southeast. On the tenth day, a watchman, who was in the crow's-nest perched high on the foremast looking through a telescope, shouted, "Bloooows! Ah bloooows!"

"Where away?" shouted back Captain Whitfield.

"Two points abaft the starboard beam."

Manjiro at once understood that a whale had been sighted. Running up on deck he saw, about two miles away, a large sperm whale lazily swimming in the trough of the sea with its broad, glossy back glistening in the sun and spouting a rainbow colored vapory jet from time to time. The ship began chasing the whale and when it shortened the distance to about fifty fathoms, it hove to and lowered four boats at once. Quickly sliding down the boat-falls as soon as the boats touched the water, the whalemen jumped into them. Each boat carried six. They began rowing in chase of the whale, which at last had become alive to its danger. Desperately it began to outdistance the pursuers.

Manjiro and those who were left in the ship breathlessly watched the boats race for the lead. Soon one of the boats, its steerer standing at the bow with a harpoon, went ahead of the other boats about two fathoms, and no sooner had the boat been tossed upon the peak of a swell than *whiz* went a harpoon and with amazing accuracy lodged in the body of the whale. The boat was at once fast to the whale. The oarsmen backed water, hot and strong, pulling and stretching the line and passing it round and round the loggerhead, but the whale began to swim away, towing the boat which soon was shooting through the churning water faster than a clipper under full sail. As soon as the whale relaxed its efforts to escape, two other boats came closing in and sent their harpoons into it so that their united lines were available even if the whale sounded. The tormented body of the whale, from which a red tide now poured,

twisted and jerked and wallowed in blood. Now half of its
body appeared on the surface like a quaint-looking rock
rising from the sea. One of the long, slender lances used by
the headsmen had pierced its heart. It shot a column of
bloody spray high into the air from its spout and then
quivered violently until at last it lay quietly, its massive
body floating at the mercy of the waves like the capsized
hull of a ship.

Manjiro and others stood on the deck, watching this
spectacle, deeply impressed. They were convinced that
their sea-bass fishing in Tosa was nothing to this thrilling
fight with a whale. They suddenly remembered a saying
in Tosa that seven ports would thrive with a catch of a
whale. If they could use the whaling methods of those
foreigners, seventy ports might thrive. I'll be a whaler
someday! said Manjiro to himself.

Manjiro and the others retired to a corner of the deck
in order to keep out of the way and curiously watched the
men at work. The whale was towed by one of the boats
to the ship and was made fast to its side, and the process
of flensing began. All the strips of the blubber were cut
in a spiral direction. When nearly the whole of the blubber
was removed in a continuous piece, it was cut into proper
lengths for the try-pot. The work went on in good order.
Men were busy at the try-pots to boil out oil, others were
filling the barrels with oil, still others were sending barrels
down to the hold by using slings and tackles. Everyone
had his own share in the work, which he quickly and skill-
fully carried out.

When the work was over, the ship headed southeast
again. A flock of gulls kept flying close behind the ship
until it was nearly dark, attracted by the odor of the whale
which had soaked into the ship.

The following day, when Manjiro was perched on the mainmast looking through a telescope, he discovered a large whale and a small one floating among the waves.

"Whales! Whales!" he shouted at the top of his voice to the men on the deck. The boats were at once lowered. Seeing the danger, the large one tried to swim away holding the small one in its breast fins, but the boats encircled it and killed it in the same way as they did the day before. However, they let the whelp whale escape unmolested. Manjiro was given a new sailor cap by the captain as a reward for discovering the whale, while Denzo, Jusuke, Toraemon and Goemon were also given similar caps as rewards for the good job they did at the slings and tackles sending down the oil barrels to the hold and cleaning the deck which had been smeared with oil.

The ship kept steadily south-southeast when finally six months' voyage brought them to a harbor called Honolulu, on Oahu Island of the Sandwich Archipelago, late in November after catching fifteen large whales. At the very sight of the land which the Japanese fishermen had so much wished to walk on, they wanted to get permission to go ashore immediately. But the captain summoned them and explained the situation in the hand language something like this:

"Now look here, I will go ashore and visit the Governor's Office in order to take steps for getting permission for your landing at the earliest date. Besides, I shall fix the place for you to stay. Now, you wait for a while before you land. Understand?"

Denzo answered, in gesture: "Captain, we understand quite well what you said just now. We'll wait."

"When you are allowed to go ashore, I am afraid, you will find it hard to make a living at first. It will be necessary for you to get some aid from the Governor's Office at least for the time being."

Although Captain Whitfield was a kindhearted man, he was straightforward and outspoken. When he happened to reprove his crewmen, he never fretted and fumed. All he did was to utter a stern word or two staring them hard in the face. The next moment he would look pleasantly nonchalant as if nothing had happened. So the crew loved him and obeyed him faithfully.

Thus Manjiro and the other four were left in the ship to wait until further notice. They often got together and discussed the problem of getting jobs when they were allowed to go ashore. They decided unanimously that they should learn the foreigners' language and they asked a sailor staying on board the ship to teach them how to say simple words. Being the oldest of them all, Denzo was found to be the slowest pupil, while Manjiro was by far the best.

Captain Whitfield seemed to have had such a lot of business to transact at Honolulu that it was nearly one month before he came to take them ashore. First they went to the Governor's Office accompanied by the captain.

The Governor was an American about fifty years of age whose name was Dr. Gerrit Parmele Judd. He had been a medical practitioner in America and had come to this island to seek his fortune. He gave up practice and became a successful politician. The popularity which he had gradually won among the islanders resulted at last in his being chosen governor of the island.

Governor Judd brought a map of the world, which Manjiro and the others had never seen before, and unfolded it before them. Pointing here and there over the map, he questioned Manjiro, using simple words.

The Governor smiled and kindly explained. "This is a

folding map. Now look here. This is the sea. This is a great land. This is an island. Well, were you born here or there?"

"We were born here," replied Manjiro pointing to an island.

Governor Judd exchanged looks with Captain Whitfield and they both nodded.

"Do you worship Buddha?"

"Yes, we do," answered Manjiro, Jusuke and Goemon in unison. Then the Governor produced from the cupboard a Japanese smoking pipe, twenty pieces of silver, one piece of gold and one piece of copper of the Kan-ei Era. "What are these?" asked he of Manjiro.

"This money," answered Manjiro, "comes from our country."

"Then do you know a place called Osaka?"

"Yes, I know."

"What sort of place is Osaka?"

"Me not saw Osaka. But Denzo here know it well. I hear Osaka a good port and a big, big place."

"Yes, Osaka is the best harbor in Japan. Now I understand quite well that you are Japanese. This long smoking pipe and the twenty-three coins were given to me fourteen years ago by men of a merchant ship belonging to Osaka. They were a bunch of good fellows and very good seamen too. Now you shall stay in this island until further notice, for I will see to it that the Government pays all your expenses while you are here. In the meantime, I'll give each of you a silver dollar as my personal gift, for you'll need some money for the present."

Manjiro and the others humbly bowed in thanks, bending low at the waist. With these silver coins in their hands, they filed out of the Governor's room and were shown into a guest room of the Office where they were served with bananas and coffee for the first time in their lives.

Thus the five men received the grants from the Government to pay the expenses for bed, board and clothing through the good offices of Captain Whitfield. He liked Manjiro in particular for his cheerfulness, politeness and willingness to learn. He would certainly regret it to his dying day, should he leave Manjiro to himself in this island. So when a question was raised whether it was all right to take Manjiro to America all the men except Manjiro were puzzled, because they were born in the same province and, after drifting together thousands of miles, had landed in a strange country and naturally found it hard to part with one of their members. Even if they were destined not to touch the soil of their beloved homeland again, it would be an unpardonable act to give up Manjiro who was no better than a helpless boy. Although Japan lay ever so far away at the dim distant end of the ocean, "a crime would run one thousand miles," as their popular saying had it. When they met the people of Nishinohama or Nakanohama of Tosa even in their dreams, how could they keep their countenance?

But Captain Whitfield was a great benefactor to them; in fact, if it had not been for him they would long since have perished. They turned the problem over and over and expressed every possible opinion. To make a long story short, they decided to leave the choice with Manjiro. Whereupon, Manjiro nonchalantly made his intention known that he would sooner go and see for himself what was the real truth of America.

Captain Whitfield, very pleased with what Manjiro had

just said, added assuringly, "I'll take good care of him, so don't you worry." Then he took Manjiro on board the ship while Denzo and the others came to the wharf to bid him farewell.

The remaining four were allowed to stay with the family of Kaukahawa, a retainer of Queen Kakaluohi. The house was a fairly large one with a thatched roof and the rooms were matted with palm leaves. In those days, the houses along the streets in Honolulu were for the most part cottages thatched with palm leaves. Only the churches were built with spired roofs. There were neither the stone walls nor the towers of a castle in Honolulu like those which they had seen at Kochi back in Tosa. Indeed, Honolulu looked far poorer and less impressive than Kochi, they thought.

But strange to say, the trees here were thick with green leaves despite the fact that it was the end of November. The harbor, facing south, was almost one mile in diameter and there were always more than fifteen whaling ships at anchor in it. At the sterns of those ships were hoisted, without exception, the flags of America, bright with stars.

Denzo and the others lived at the Government's expense until the next summer, by which time they had become somewhat familiar with the language and the custom of the place so that they were able to go on errands and do simple chores. Anyway, as they did not like to remain under the Government's care indefinitely, they went to see Governor Judd, hoping he would assign to them some jobs, but the former medical man kindly said, "You need not work nor worry about anything at all. You are under Government protection and you can stay here at the expense of the Government."

So they let another year pass in this way, but at last they felt they could no longer go on like this, and again they applied to the Governor for some work. Finally, Denzo and his brother Goemon were employed temporarily as servants at the houses of the Governor's relatives and friends, their jobs being drawing water, hewing wood, carrying lunch boxes, and cleaning the house. Toraemon became an apprentice to a carpenter through the good offices of the Governor, while Jusuke was suffering from a relapse of his wounded foot. His condition was steadily worsening.

TO
FAIRHAVEN,
MASS.

WHILE the *John Howland* carrying Manjiro kept steadily south, Captain Whitfield grew to like the boy, who was good-natured and a willing and hard worker, and before long treated him like his own son. The captain decided to call him John Mung as his name Manjiro was too much for the sailors. Having lost his father when a mere child, Manjiro, hungering for fatherly love, became firmly attached to this stern but kind captain. He was brighter than the others, he had picked up English and spoke it with considerable ease. He studied hard in his spare moments and soon he was able to write some simple English words. He found it easier to learn the English alphabet, which was much simpler than the Japanese one. The captain loved John Mung all the more and the crew, too, began to like the boy and treated him kindly and called him by his new name.

He certainly missed the fellow countrymen with whom he had parted at Honolulu but as the captain was kind and there were on the ship three teen-age sailors — La Fayette Wilcox, for instance, was only sixteen — with whom he could be friendly, he was not lonely except when he thought of his home. Moreover, the life on the whaling ship was so exciting that he had little time to think of his home.

The ship touched at an equatorial island among the Kingsmill Group to get a fresh supply of fuel and water. It was a small island somewhat over two miles in circumference and its inhabitants were all black people who covered only their loins with the leaves of trees. Some of them came to the ship in their canoes to sell bows and arrows. The crew gave them only small pieces of scrap iron or other odds and ends in exchange for those weapons.

The ship engaged in whaling in the waters of the Kingsmill Group and in March, 1842, it arrived at Spanish Guam Island which lay due south of the Ogasawara Islands. John Mung set foot on the island with several crew members. It was a large island which seemed about ten miles in circumference, and the bay where a good harbor lay was over three miles across. The houses of the natives which numbered about three hundred were thatched with palm leaves, like the houses in Honolulu.

Leaving Guam Island at the end of April, the ship went up north and after coasting along only about one hundred miles off the coast of Japan, she changed her course toward the south-southeast and reached Emirau Island, a British territory, at the end of November. It was an island also about eight miles in circumference with about three hundred thatched houses. They stayed here about one month and then headed southwest until they reached Guam Island again in February of the next year. Thus the ship went in every direction in her voyage, making a large circle in the Pacific Ocean west of Oahu.

After staying for one month at Guam, the *John Howland* set sail in a south-southeasterly direction and the end of April that year saw the ship sail via Cape Horn, and go up north. At last, on May 7, 1843, the *John Howland*, completing its long, long voyage of three years and seven months, entered the port of New Bedford, Massachusetts.

The sailors, who had been up before daybreak while the *John Howland*, weather-beaten, heavy with whale oil, was steadily plowing through the calm sea of Buzzards Bay, were all excited at this long-awaited homecoming, but perhaps no one was so excited as the sixteen-year-old Japanese boy, who was determined to see the New World with his own eyes. By the time the ship sailed between Palmer's Island and Fort Phoenix and dropped anchor at last in New Bedford Harbor, the sun was beginning to shine through the early morning mist, on the wings of the gulls flying around the ship, and on its main royal mast. Soon Captain Whitfield appeared on the deck where Manjiro had kept leaning over the bulwarks to watch the harbor and the town, where about thirty ships of all types lay at anchor and where a town of big painted strange-looking houses and church steeples was in full view on this bright May morning.

"We've at last come home, John Mung!" said the captain, coming beside him.

"I can't believe my eyes, Captain!" said Manjiro.

"This is New Bedford."

"It's like a dream!"

"We'll soon go ashore, John Mung."

"I can hardly wait," said Manjiro excitedly. "What are those big houses, Captain?"

"That's the custom house and that's a church, if you know what they are."

"Your house, Captain, can you see it?"

"Nay, not from here; it's in Fairhaven on the other side of this river."

"Is that a river? Looks like the sea."

"Aye, that is the Acushnet River, John Mung."

Soon the ship was visited by a party of relief sailors coming in a rowboat from the shore; and Captain Whitfield, John Mung, and the other crewmen at once went ashore in the boat that had just been made vacant, each carrying a seaman's bag bulging with things from foreign countries. They were happy; their eyes shining in their haggard faces. They had been working hard on the homeward-bound ship, because the original crew of twenty-seven men had been reduced to about fifteen; some had left the ship at Calio, some at Ascension and other places. On the wharf, a crowd of friends, relatives and families welcomed them but Captain Whitfield felt lonely because he was a widower. He at once took John around the town.

The boy from the lonely fishing village in Tosa had never seen such a bustling town in his life, not even in his dreams; and simply dumfounded, he stared at everything openmouthed. The wharves, warehouses, churches, offices, stores, houses, streets and parks which he saw for the first time in his life, took his breath away, and made his feet difficult to move. But when he saw women walking along the streets in bonnets, muslin ruffs and hoop skirts, balancing their pink, white, blue, green parasols, with the deep embroidered border, it was too much even for his curiosity.

Captain Whitfield, John Mung, and some of the seamen went to the Seamen's Bethel and offered prayers of thanks for their safe return "through the peril of the deep." John Mung did not understand very well the meaning of the prayers, but he was impressed by the singing of hymns and the sound of the organ. While they were praying, he was thinking of his widowed mother saying the *sutra* in the village temple far away somewhere in the world.

Then John Mung, still dazed and breathless, accompanied by Captain Whitfield, crossed a mile-long bridge spanning the Acushnet River and reached Fairhaven where the captain lived. Fairhaven which was on New Bedford Harbor was also a prosperous town full of fine houses, though it was not so big and thriving with the whaling industry as New Bedford. As Captain Whitfield was a widower, his house had been left vacant and unlivable during his absence and although he loved John like a son, he could not have the boy live with him in his own house. Therefore, he asked one of the townsmen by the name of Eben Akin who had been a third officer of a whaling ship under Captain Whitfield to let John stay with his family. In the neighborhood, there lived together three sisters and the middle one, Jane Allen, was teaching at the Stone School in Farm Lane, a private school where she had about thirty pupils. One day Mr. Eben Akin asked John Mung whether he would like to go to school. John answered that he wanted to do so by all means. As it was unlikely that he would be able to return to Japan in the near future, he thought he should get some education in America.

John Mung went to school for the first time in his life.

In a large paneled room, about thirty feet square, stood
rows of desks and chairs. About thirty pupils sat at those
desks having a lesson in reading. The teacher stood on the
platform, writing on the blackboard with a piece of chalk.
The pupils at first kept the strange freshman at a respect-
ful distance, but before long, friendship prevailed and they
began to play with him and to treat him kindly as one of
their number. John Mung stayed on with Mr. Akin and
went to school every morning, returning home late in the
afternoon. As he was a great lover of books, Miss Jane
Allen used to lend him many useful books so that he could
read them in his spare time.

Soon after John Mung joined the family of Mr. Eben
Akin, Captain Whitfield went to New York to sell the
whale oil which the *John Howland* had brought back from
the long whaling expedition. Not only did he conclude a
very profitable business deal but he also remarried in New
York, on May 31 of that year. He married Miss Albertina
B. Keith of Bridgewater, Massachusetts, and returned home
in the height of happiness with his beautiful bride. Then
he purchased a fourteen-acre farm with some buildings in
Sconticut Neck, a mile or so from Fairhaven, for one
thousand dollars from one Alice P. Fuller. There they established their new home in a house they built, to which
John Mung, after a while, came to live to make himself
useful in doing the household chores. On the farm Captain
and Mrs. Whitfield, with the help of John Mung and
a hired farmhand, kept several cows, horses, pigs, and about
one hundred chickens and also raised wheat, corn, potatoes,
grapes and so on.

It is told that, as a person of consequence in the town,
Captain Whitfield had his own private pew in one of the

three churches. One Sunday morning Manjiro went to church with him and sat beside him in that pew. One of the deacons of the church, who had been horrified, came to see Captain Whitfield after a few weeks and told him that the Japanese boy would have to sit in the pew for Negroes, because some of the members had objected to having Manjiro sit in the captain's pew. Captain Whitfield bowed politely and made no reply, although he wanted to say, "As long as I live, I shall never attend your church." Immediately he took a pew in another church but soon met with the same result.

Before long, the captain found that a Unitarian Church was willing to admit John Mung into the fold, so that he decided to take the boy to this church every Sunday. Eventually the captain and his family became its members. The church's principal supporter was Mr. Warren Delano, Sr., who was an influential townsman and the great-grandfather of the late Franklin Delano Roosevelt, who once wrote, "I well remember my grandfather telling me all about the little Japanese boy who went to school in Fairhaven and who went to church from time to time with the Delano family."

Once he was deeply moved when he heard a sermon in which the pastor said that even a humble man was often called upon to do an important job. He did not clearly understand what was meant by being "poor in spirit" though the pastor talked about it at some length. He was encouraged, and filled with hope, however, when the pastor said that many men of humble birth proved to be capable of doing great service to the world. He was astonished when he was told that one of the greatest followers of the Lord was a fisherman. When the sermon was over, he said to himself, I am glad that a fisherman's blood is in me. What can I do when I am a man?

Manjiro was happy in this small New England town because, as the captain's foster son, he was allowed to do whatever was normal for any Fairhaven boy of that period, but sometimes he felt very lonely thinking of his poor widowed mother. Then he would take out a small tattered cotton kimono which his mother had made for him and bury his face in it and sob. He would wipe his tears with it and talk to it in Japanese as if he had been talking to his mother. He thought then as if his mother had been there to cheer him up because he knew that it was his mother who had made it for him and the only thing he had in his possession to remember her by. He always said on such occasions, "Mother, I will come back to you someday!"

One day, Job C. Trippe, who was a classmate of John Mung, happened to come into the latter's room and found him crying with his face buried in the small tattered kimono. When John told him why he was crying in such a manner, Job Trippe began to cry and they both cried together for some time. But when he suddenly noticed that John Mung's head was sticking out of a big hole in the kimono, he began to laugh and they both laughed together. Much impressed by Manjiro's attachment for his mother, Job Trippe wrote a few days later a very touching composition on the theme of mother love. Those who heard him read this composition in class were deeply moved.

When John Mung came to live with Captain and Mrs. Whitfield at the Sconticut Neck farm, he lived in a home for the first time in his life. When a small boy, he had lost his father, and his mother was poor. She used to go down to the beach every day to help the fishermen draw dragnets to get a few small fish for her children. But in Sconticut Neck, he lived with his foster father and mother who were always kind to him, although like any other New England parents, they were by no means soft. At last, he could satisfy his hunger for fatherly love from Captain Whitfield. The three often worked together on the farm and he was as happy as a boy could be. He worked hard and they liked him.

On Fourth of July he was taken by Captain Whitfield to Fairhaven to see the sham fight and the parade, which he always recalled and talked about even before the Japanese officials. In Sconticut Neck, he observed the quaint custom of Halloween and celebrated Christmas with the tree, candles, presents, turkey dinner and carols in its New England setting.

In Sconticut Neck he soon found that there were several playmates with whom he could go fishing when he was not too busy farming or reading books. He made many friends. On May Day, John Mung and other children went a-Maying before sunrise in the nearby field to gather wild flowers and tree branches, and they returned to the village in triumph, John Mung carrying the Maypole. It was told by the late Mrs. Eldridge G. Morton that on a May Day when she was still a small child, John Mung hung a May basket on her door with the following verse:

> *Tis in the silly night*
> *A basket you've got hung.*
> *Get up! Strike a light!*
> *And see me run.*

to which he added, "But no chase me." John Mung followed this and many other New England customs of the day and thoroughly enjoyed them even if he did not understand them very well.

He continued to read books when he was free from the work in the field or at the cowshed, so that Captain Whitfield was more and more impressed by the boy's strong desire to learn. Mr. Louis Bartlett, a mathematician, who managed school at 42 Spring Street, was also impressed by the diligence and love of learning of this boy and said that he would teach John Mung mathematics and surveying, if he had any desire to learn. The young man readily became one of the pupils of Mr. Bartlett in February, 1844, and studied mathematics, surveying, reading and writing in his spare hours and proved to be the brightest student in the class. In June of that year, Captain Whitfield went whaling again from the port of New Bedford on board the *William Eliza* without John Mung, because not only was his service needed around the farm but the captain thought that the boy's education should not be interrupted.

The work in the field was finished for the winter, and John Mung could have lived a fairly easy life doing nothing in particular at Captain Whitfield's if he wanted to do so. He was too grateful to merely bask in the motherly care of Mrs. Whitfield, nor could he reconcile himself to the idea of idling away his time. Thinking of his future, he wanted to use this time to learn some trade while he could, so he became in February, 1845, an apprentice to a cooper named Mr. Huzzy, a manufacturer of whale-oil barrels, whose trade was considered a respectable one in the whaling community in those days. There were two other apprentices in the house of Mr. Huzzy, but as the work was too hard and the food too bad, they soon left the house without giving any notice. John Mung, however, stayed on patiently.

While he worked hard as the cooper's apprentice, he read books and attended Mr. Bartlett's school whenever he had time to spare.

In the summer of that year when the work at the Sconticut Neck farm was in full swing, he returned to it to be a farmhand again. The early autumn saw him return to Mr. Huzzy, but before long he became ill, having overworked himself, and had to return to Sconticut Neck in October. When he became quite well again under the care of Mrs. Whitfield, he resumed his studies of mathematics and navigation, whenever he was not too busy on the farm. But sometimes when he thought of the thrill of chasing whales in the broad open sea, he could not help thinking that the job of taking care of pigs was rather boring.

He was then a lad of nineteen, feeling a nostalgia for the sea. He wanted, moreover, to put into practice on the ship the knowledge of navigation and surveying he had acquired from Mr. Bartlett. But the opportunity to do so did not present itself at that time, so he decided in February, 1846, to go back to Mr. Huzzy's to continue his apprenticeship in the cooper's trade.

It happened that a whaler from New York named Ira Davis, who was once the harpooner on the *John Howland*, came to Fairhaven in order to organize a crew for the *Franklin*, which was bound for the Pacific under his captainship. He went to see John Mung and asked him to join his crew; he had already been told by Isachar Akin, whom he also asked to sail on the *Franklin*, about the courage and skill which John Mung had demonstrated on the *John Howland*.

Upon learning that his former shipmate, Isachar Akin, had consented to the proposal and that he would be appointed first officer, John Mung accepted the offer at once, since it seemed to be the very thing for which he had been waiting all this while. He thought it might be a good chance to return to Japan. He went to see Mrs. Whitfield immediately and told her that he had decided to go whaling on the *Franklin,* and asked her approval. But he did not breathe a word about any possibility of his returning to Japan.

"I'm indeed glad to hear that, and I'm proud of you, John, and I'm sure Captain Whitfield would have been pleased to hear it. You ain't a small boy any more, and I reckon Mr. Bartlett learned you a thing or two about sailing a ship and whaling. You'll make a good whaler like my husband some day, I'm telling you. Take good care of yourself, John, and God bless you!"

"Thank you, Mrs. Whitfield. I like it here very much. I like the people here. You have been kind to me; and the captain . . . Oh, how can I thank him enough? I'll miss you, and Fairhaven, and Sconticut Neck, but I want to go to sea. Perhaps, I may be able to see the captain, if the *William Eliza* and the *Franklin* happen to meet somewhere in the Pacific Ocean. How I long to see him!"

John Mung said goodbye again and again to Mrs. Whitfield and picked up William, the baby, from the floor and fondled him for a few minutes before he took leave of the Sconticut Neck farm. Then he went on board the *Franklin* without delay.

The *Franklin* was a ship of 273 tons. She was about 100 feet long and carried a crew of twenty-four. John Mung soon found to his great joy that ten of them were from the New Bedford area, some of whom he already knew; he found also that twelve of them were teen-agers, the youngest only fifteen. On May 15, 1846, the ship weighed anchor from New Bedford and sailed into Boston Harbor, where it stayed for three days. War was in the air in Boston Harbor, with the loaded cannons on the fortified islands menacingly pointing toward the sea and frigates busily keeping watch against possible emergency. The war with Mexico had already started.

The *Franklin* headed out east across the Atlantic, touched at Fayal Island in the Azores and stayed there for two days; then it headed south and reached São Thiago of the Cape Verde Islands where they bought pigs and fuel from the natives. Going farther south, the ship called at the Cape of Good Hope and continued her voyage. One day when the ship was sailing near British Guiana, a sailor who was watching from the topmast shrouds suddenly shouted, "A giant turtle!" He pointed to the trough of the sea about fifteen fathoms away from the starboard. "There it is!" cried the men on the deck. *Whiz!* went a harpoon from one of them but it fell short of the mark. Another one flew and this time it lodged deep in the body of the ten-foot monster turtle, which struggled so wildly and fiercely that it was impossible to pull the rope. Manjiro at once took off his clothes, jumped into the sea and swam over to the struggling turtle. Sitting astride it he plunged a dagger into its neck. This brave action on his part won the great admiration of the entire crew.

John Mung had ample opportunity to use the nautical instruments on the *Franklin*, such as the compasses, sextants, chronometers and so on, and successfully to employ the art of navigation which he had learned from Mr. Bartlett. He quickly grasped how to steer a big ship, how to find out the ship's position and many other things which a navigator should know. He often gave time to survey the coast lines or the sea for the sake of practice. He was admired by all the sailors of the *Franklin* for the skill which he ably demonstrated.

The ship sailed on, catching whales in the waters of Sumatra and Java, and in February, 1847, reached Kupang on Timor Island, which belonged to the Portuguese. Kupang, however, was a Dutch town of about two hundred houses, with a good port situated at the end of the bay which stretched ten miles deep into the land. While the *Franklin* was staying in this port for thirty days, John Mung often went ashore to see the town where Dutchmen lived among the natives.

This voyage proved to be a great eye opener for John Mung. At the ports of call, as a young man who was determined to see the world for himself, he met many men and women of different races, saw many scenes and experienced many things. The ship set sail from Kupang and next went to New Ireland in the Bismarck Archipelago where John Mung saw the cannibals with their faces smeared with clay and their hair powdered white, but he could hardly tell whether they were men or women. The sailors tried to get the cannibals' shields and other weapons but since they had to run a risk of being caught and devoured, they left those deadly tools with the cannibals.

Then the *Franklin* caught whales in the waters of the Solomon Islands but she had to stay at one of the islands for a few days to undergo some repairs, after which she headed north and reached Guam in March, 1847. Here John Mung wrote a letter to Captain Whitfield.

Guam, March 12, 1847

Respected Friend:

I will take the pen to write you a few lines and let you know that I am well and hope you were the same. First thing I will tell you about the home, then time I left. Well, sir, your boy William is well all summer but the cold weather sets in he will . . . smart, a little cunning creature I ever saw before. He will cry after me just as quick as he would to his mother. Your wife and Amelia and Mr. Bonney's family and your neighborhoods they all well when I saw them. I did went to Mr. Huzzeys and stayed there about six months and then I left them . . .

He goes on to pay a tribute to Mrs. Whitfield, who was a considerate, hard-working and respectable person and then he said that he believed that the captain was his best friend in all the world next to great God. He also expressed his intention to land in Ryukyu, if possible, and do his best to open a port there to supply necessaries to foreign whaling ships. He left this letter, together with Mrs. Whitfield's letter, addressed to her husband in Guam so that he might pick them up when he entered the port. After a month's stay at Guam, the ship left the island and caught more whales in the East China Sea. She sailed by the coast of Taiwan and reached the Ryukyu Islands.

John Mung always kept handy a kimono in which he wanted to return to his native land, but his heart failed him when the opportunity to go ashore presented itself. Some of the men lowered a boat and approached a seaside village where they bartered four rolls of calico for two cows. But they feared that if they stayed too long on the island they might get into some trouble. In fact, they saw several islanders come toward them menacingly, so they cut the boat from her moorings and returned hastily to the ship. Now the ship headed east and went near the lonely island on which John Mung and the others had been stranded. From the entries in the logbook of the *John Howland* he had gathered that the island was in all probability Torishima of the Hachijo Islands. There they caught more whales and angled for fish. In August of that year, when the *Franklin* was sailing a hundred and sixty miles off the coast of North Japan, she met unexpectedly with about twenty Japanese fishing boats.

This particular part of the sea seemed to have taken on a different color because of a large school of bonito riding on the Black Current of the Pacific Ocean. The fishermen in the boats felt almost dizzy, so busy were they in hauling in their catch. The *Franklin* lowered her sails in order to take her share in this heavy haul. Everyone took out his tackle and fished for bonito until about two hundred of them were hooked out of the water. Just then two Japanese boats came toward the *Franklin*, perhaps resenting that she was intruding on their point of vantage. John Mung put on his kimono and wrapped a headband around his head in the Japanese style and stood on the deck calling out to the boats as loud as he could.

"Where do you come from? Those are Japanese boats, I take it. What province do they belong to?"

John Mung spoke Japanese for the first time in many years. Not in a dream but in a full waking moment he shouted his mother tongue as loudly as he pleased to his fellow countrymen. But he felt ashamed of himself to find that he was tongue-tied and had forgotten some Japanese words.

"What part of Japan do those boats come from, eh? Are they from Tosa?"

"Sundai, Sundai," was the answer from the boats.

"Sunday?" wondered John Mung. "Why? This is not Sunday."

Then it dawned on him that they had pronounced the name Sendai (a town in North Japan) in their dialect.

John Mung lowered a boat at once and carrying with him a present of two boxes of bread, rowed toward the fishing boats from "Sundai," until the bow of his boat almost touched the side of one of the Japanese boats. He offered a few loaves of bread to the fishermen from "Sundai" which they accepted suspiciously and only stared at for a moment, unable to make head or tail of them, because they had never seen bread before. John Mung spoke to a young man who was apparently the headman.

"Are your boats going to Tosa?"

The young man looked puzzled as if he could not understand John Mung's Tosa accent.

"I don't know," was the answer.

"Then don't you know whether there is a boat that goes to Tosa?"

"I don't know," was again the answer of the young man.

"Can't you understand what I say? Tell me if any of your boats is going to Tosa."

"I don't know," repeated the young fisherman and taking out some bonito that he had kept in storage, he offered them in return for the present, saying, "Katsuo!"

It was possible that they acted as if they could not understand very well what John Mung said because they wanted to have nothing to do with a stranger, fearing they might get into trouble. John Mung gave up any further attempt to make himself understood and signed as much as to say, "We have caught enough bonito, so I must decline your offer with due thanks." Seeing that it was no use trying to make further negotiations, he returned to the ship a disappointed man. He stood on the deck blankly staring at the sea until someone drew his attention to the headband which he had forgotten to take off.

Most of the men in the ship who had been curiously watching John Mung negotiate with the Japanese fishermen felt sorry to know that his hope of returning to Tosa in one of those boats had been dashed.

AN
EMPTY HOPE

THE *Franklin* steadily took a southeast course for many days on end, making unusually good headway before the wind. In October, 1847, she entered the port of Honolulu and lay at anchor for about a month during which the ship took in fuel and fresh water. It was seven long years since John Mung bade farewell to Denzo and the others in Honolulu.

He waited patiently for shore leave, and as soon as it was granted he went to look for them. On inquiring of an office clerk and a tailor whom he had known as to the whereabouts of Denzo and the other Japanese, he was told that Denzo and his brother had gone home to Japan, that Jusuke had died, and only Toraemon was still staying there as an apprentice to a carpenter. He proceeded at once to the carpenter's house, where he found Toraemon busily sawing a timber with a large saw.

Greatly surprised at the sight of John Mung, Toraemon said, "Oh! Manjiro Nushi!" Then he said in English, "This is, indeed, an unexpected meeting. What brought you here?"

John Mung said, "Oh! Tora Nushi!" and continued also in English, "I am glad to find you well. I came here a couple of days ago in a whaleship called the *Franklin* and heard that you were still here and that Den Nushi and Goemon Nushi had gone back to Japan. I also heard that Jusuke was dead and gone. Poor man!"

"Yes, poor man!" said Toraemon. "I feel as if my heart would break when I think of him. 'I may die in this strange land but my spirit will go back to my old country.' That was what he said just before he breathed his last. I remember, it was a mighty windy day in January of last year when he passed away. Den Nushi and Goemon Nushi sailed to Japan on the *Colorado* at the end of October, last year. Indeed, I wanted to go back with them, but I did not dare to go in that ship because I was told that Captain Cox was a devil if ever a man was. I kind of feared I might get into some trouble if I sailed with that skipper. Now, I've said enough for the present. Let me hear from you all about what you've done since you left."

John Mung began to tell his long story, how he had been taken to America by Captain Whitfield, how he had spent the last seven years; how he had been employed on a whaling ship and how he had at last come to this place. As it was the first reunion in many years they both had many things to talk about.

About twenty days went by, when one day the carpenter,

returning in a hurry from the town, said, "Toraemon, I met just now a sailor who told me that the *Colorado* had just made port. He also said that he had seen Denzo and the other Japanese still in the ship."

It was such an unexpected piece of news that Toraemon could not believe his ears at first. He went to see Manjiro at once and broke the news. Then they ran together to the harbor where they saw the *Colorado* at anchor, and hiring a boat at once, they rowed to the ship and went on board. Sure enough, they found Denzo and his brother standing on the deck.

Denzo began to tell the story of his last seven years to John Mung: He and his brother lived at first under the care of Governor Judd, but feeling too proud to accept charity, they soon decided to work. Inexperienced in any trade and having no capital to buy land, they managed to make a living as servants or day laborers for the relatives and friends of Governor Judd. As for Jusuke, his condition was gradually getting worse, so that he was at last sent along with his two brothers to the house of Pookun in a village called Kualoa, six miles away, to get special medical treatment from a famous doctor there. Jusuke died in January, 1845, at the age of thirty-one, in spite of all efforts to cure him. A funeral service was held for him at the Kualoa Church by his brothers, Pookun and a few other friends of the deceased. He was buried in the graveyard of his former master's family, which was not far from Kualoa. Denzo took his brother's death to heart and became so dejected that Pookun had to look after him while his brother Goemon stayed at the mission house there to work as a servant.

Once when Queen Kakaluohi came to this village on her annual tour of inspection, escorted by the chief official

Tuwanahawa, they stopped at Pookun's house where Denzo was staying. Tuwanahawa told them that it was the queen's wish to inquire after his and his brother's health and to know that everything was all right with them. They thanked the queen for her kindness and then told the chief official how they had been getting along on the island and expressed their wish to make a living by farming and fishing, if that were possible. A few days later Tuwanahawa told Denzo and his brother, "You shall have the land to farm." Realizing that the queen must have granted their wish, Denzo asked the chief official to take steps to express their gratitude to her.

Denzo and his brother built a house of their own on the newly granted land by the sea, and busied themselves farming and fishing. They made themselves fishing tackle after that of Tosa and fished chiefly for bonito. They sold their catch at the markets in Honolulu. They were so skillful that either of them could catch fifty bonito while a native of the island could get only ten. Their farm land, warmed by the sun, yielded a good harvest of potatoes. In the back yard they kept pigs for the first time in their lives, according to the custom of the natives. Moreover, as they were exempted from all taxes, they were able to live as comfortably as they could wish. When Goemon had nothing to do in the field or in the sea, he often went to work as a servant for a certain missionary.

One Sunday morning, when a preaching meeting of this missionary was over, someone in the congregation shouted, "Well, Goemon! Can you recognize me?"

"How could I have forgotten you?" said Goemon. "To be sure, you are Captain Whitfield who saved our lives. We always remember you with heart and soul."

Captain Whitfield, looking very pleased, laughed heartily and then asked Goemon how his friends had been getting along. Goemon told the captain all he and his friends had done since they saw him last but when he told that Jusuke had died, the captain looked very sad and said, "Bless his heart, poor Jusuke! How badly he must have wanted to go back to Japan before he died!"

In tears the captain and Goemon went to visit the grave of Jusuke. Later the captain suddenly said, "I can help you go back to Japan, if you still want to go. Mr. Cox, who was once a crew member of the *Howland*, is now the captain of a whaling ship called *Colorado*, which is about to leave for Japanese waters. If you want to go back, I can ask him to take you to your country in that ship. So you'd better get ready to sail, if that is your wish. You may depend upon it, he is a very nice man, and I am sure he will take good care of you. By the way, John Mung is living quite happily in Fairhaven. He is doing fine at school."

Then the captain and Goemon went together to Denzo's cottage on the seaside, which was a small ramshackle affair with not a single chair to sit on. When Denzo saw the captain and Goemon, he was so glad that he could hardly speak. He invited them to sit on two barrels which were standing on the dirt floor. Although the captain did not like the look of the shabby cottage and its surroundings, he suddenly said, looking toward the sea, "Well, well, what a nice and simple life this is!" He then told Denzo about his plan of arranging their free passage to Japan. He asked Denzo to come to the harbor to talk the matter over if he wanted to return to Japan. Before he left the cottage, he gave Denzo and his brother two silver coins each.

On the following day Goemon, Denzo and his brother

went to the harbor to see Captain Whitfield. He eyed their clothes disapprovingly and said, "I'm afraid you cannot go back to your country in those clothes. You'd better put these on when you go." Then the captain gave each of them a suit of woolen clothes, a pair of shoes, a hat and a few shirts. Goemon packed them together into a bundle and carrying it on a pole over his shoulder as Japanese farmers did, he returned to his seaside cottage. Denzo and Goemon were overjoyed and at once went to Honolulu to see Toraemon.

"Tora Nushi! We have good news for you. At last we can go home." They explained the matter in detail and tried to talk him into returning to Japan.

Denzo and the other two went to see their friends in Honolulu to say goodbye. Dr. Judd and the missionary gave them some money, clothes and other presents, wishing them good luck. Some of their friends exchanged words of parting with tears in their eyes, because they had become very good friends by then.

Returning to the seaside cottage, Denzo and his brother cheerfully set about the preparations for their voyage home. They could not contain the joy of going home after so many years of loneliness in a strange country. Although they found that the fields in which they had sweated so hard were something they could not part with so easily, they offered the potatoes and corn in the field to the neighbors and returned the land to Twanahawa. Six chickens, four ducks, and two pigs, which they had kept, were given as presents to Captain Whitfield.

Captain Whitfield again asked Mr. Cox to look after the three men just before the *Colorado* set sail. The three went on board, while Captain Whitfield came to see them off.

But just as the ship was weighing anchor, ready to set sail, Toraemon changed his mind.

"I'm not going back," he blurted out. Denzo, surprised out of his wits, told him persuasively that if he did not return now, most likely he'd never return. Whereupon, Toraemon said that Captain Cox was a "son of a dog" and would bring a great deal of trouble to them in the ship. He would not listen to any of Denzo's advice and went ashore all by himself. It seemed that he had harbored some suspicion about the character of Mr. Cox.

The *Colorado* left Honolulu late in November and, going south, engaged in whaling in the waters of the South Sea Islands, finally putting in at Guam Island to spend the year's end. Then she headed north, coming close to Hachijo Island the early part of March, but the sea was too rough to lower a boat. So, passing about ten miles off the island, she headed northeast and kept her course along the coast of Boshu. The ship then came so near the shore of what appeared to be Matsumae that it came into view very clearly. Captain Cox told Denzo that the cape in sight was Matsumae, and brought the ship to within four miles of the coast. Then the captain, Denzo, his brother and six men went ashore in a boat at the northern part of the cape. They set out to look for a village or a house. They found two small vacant huts. Inside one of them they found Japanese sandals and straw raincoats hanging on the wall. A pair of well-used straw shoes covered with dry dust was on the dirt floor. The ashes in the fireplace seemed dead and cold. "Ohi! Ohi!" Denzo and his brother shouted at the top of their lungs, but neither a human voice nor an echo was heard in answer to the shout. At the back of the house they found a small patch planted with taro. There was no doubt that this was Japanese territory but not a living soul was to be found anywhere. They went up a hill, made a bonfire and waited for a long time, but no one came.

"This," said Captain Cox at last, "is a lonely place, no better than an uncharted island. To stay here is out of the question. Denzo, I'll let you go ashore at a more suitable place, so you'd better come along with us to the ship for now."

When Denzo and his brother came ashore, they believed that they had come at last to the land they had dreamed about so often, after so many years of waiting. So they begged the captain to be left alone on this island.

"If I left you alone here at this lonely place," said he, "how could I explain myself to Captain Whitfield who asked me to look after you and see you safely returned to Japan? For heaven's sake, don't stay in such a deserted place. I'm sure we'll find many other places more suitable to land."

"Please," implored Denzo, "we beg of you, Captain, leave us alone here." They both clasped their hands over their heads and bowed humbly.

"I will do nothing of the kind," said the captain in flat refusal. So at last, Denzo and his brother had to return to the ship, sad and disappointed. The *Colorado* then went up north and caught more whales in the eastern waters of the Aleutian Islands, where they had to spend forty stormy, sunless days. They returned to Honolulu the early part of August, catching twenty-three whales in all.

Denzo told the above story to John Mung and said that he and his brother had just returned to Honolulu from the voyage that very day. When Denzo's story was over, John Mung put in, "I think Mr. Cox is not so black as Tora Nushi paints him."

"Well," insisted Toraemon, "I still think that he is a blackhearted man all right."

Judging from what Denzo had said, it seemed as if Mr. Cox might have tricked Denzo and his brother into boarding the *Colorado,* as Toraemon had suspected, and let them work for nothing. However, it was possible at the same time that he knew full well the strict isolation policy of Japan at that time and the possible consequences that might ensue from violating it. He himself had landed in an obscure nook of Matsumae and had tried to find a house and had made a bonfire on a hill in an attempt to see Denzo and his brother returned safely among their men. After all, he was a good man who dared not abandon the two men in that lonely place, particularly when he had been asked by Captain Whitfield to be kind to them.

The *Franklin* carrying John Mung was setting sail any time then, so giving up the talk that seemed to know no end, he said goodbye to them, wishing them good luck till they should meet again.

Denzo and Goemon, on returning to Honolulu, visited all their former friends who had been kind enough to give them presents when they were leaving town before and told how their attempt to return to Japan had failed, and how they had to return to Honolulu. They asked their former friends to continue to be kind to them, and retired to a place called Maeha, about ten miles from Honolulu, and settled down there as humble peasants.

IN

THE

GOLD RUSH

THE *Franklin* left Honolulu for the South Seas and anchored on November 6, 1847, at Guam. About this time,
Captain Ira Davis became insane and committed all sorts of
violent acts so that the crew decided to take him to Manila
on Luzon Island. The ship continued whaling during this
voyage until she made port at Manila the latter part of May.

As there was an American consulate in Manila, some of
the members of the crew went to see the consul, explained
the matter to him and asked his advice. As a result, it was
decided that the insane captain should be returned to
America on a transport. John Mung often went ashore on
official business and whenever he found time to spare, he
hung about the town. It was full of people of different
races and nationalities, including Americans, Spaniards,

Dutchmen, Englishmen, Hindoos, Chinese, Filipinos, and others, who mingled together so that the place seemed like an emporium of races.

The *Franklin* having been thus bereft of her captain, Mr. Isachar Akin, first officer, became acting captain. John Mung was chosen second officer unanimously by the crew, who had been admiring his personality and the pluck and skill with which he caught whales.

Leaving Manila in July, the *Franklin* went to the waters of Batangas, Taiwan and the Ryukyu Islands where it engaged in whaling before it turned back to Guam. Getting a supply of fuel and water at this island, the ship again put to sea and in October she entered Honolulu. Before she left the port for the last whaling voyage and for home, John Mung wrote the following letter. It clearly shows that he had experienced the Christian faith which no doubt he had learned from Captain Whitfield:

> Honolulu,
> Oct. 30th, 1848

Oh! Captain how can I forget your kindness. When can I pay for your fatherly treatment. Thank God ten thousand times and never will forget.

I was sorry your ship being leaky and oblige you into the port before your season, however, God will see all this. I often offer prayers to God to give you the success should it please to God. Your success will under the divine providence in a great measure depend upon your own conduct. The God will direct you into the straitest [?] path of the sea. Hope you return safe and self preservation. I and my good Albertina and Amelin find them injoying the health and happiness. We were lying with 700 bbls. of sperm oil and have to go another season on the line.

July 9th had the gam with Captain Woodard I followed

him up on the deck inquire for home and find the death of my boy William Henry [Captain Whitfield's son]. I was very sorry every time think about William Henry. Give my best respects to all your friends and your kind neighbors, and my affection your wife Amelin and Mr. Bonney family. Tell them what quarter of the world that I am in.

I never can forget kindness they have done to me. It is hard thing for me to join the words together therefore come to close.

JOHN MUNG

After leaving this island and crossing the Indian Ocean, the ship sailed off the coast of Madagascar late in May via the Cape of Good Hope. She sailed into the Atlantic and at last came back to the port of New Bedford in August of that year. It was a long voyage, extending over a period of three years and putting a girdle round the globe. The catch of whales during this long voyage numbered about five hundred, and several thousand barrels of whale oil came into their possession.

John Mung earned three hundred and fifty dollars as his share of the profit and returned to the house of Captain Whitfield at Fairhaven, his second home. The captain, who had also returned home from the sea a few days before, was waiting for him. He thought that the captain might scold him for running away from home during his absence, but the captain didn't say a word about it. On the contrary, he congratulated John Mung upon his successful whaling voyage and also upon his having been appointed second officer of the *Franklin*. John Mung told the captain how he accidentally had met Denzo, Goemon, and Toraemon, and how they had tried in vain to return to Japan. Whereupon the captain said that the place where they had landed and which they thought was Matsumae, was in all probability not Matsumae after all. He said that a large number of islands were lying like steppingstones north of Matsumae and here and there on these islands there were cottages built by Japanese settlers. It must have been those cabins that Denzo and the others found there. And Captain Whitfield concluded that there was nothing wrong with the step taken by Mr. Cox under the circumstances.

In 1848, while John Mung was on a long whaling voyage, America was stirred by the discovery of gold in California. The Gold Rush began. Upon his return to Fairhaven, the thought of adventure haunted his mind. Why not go to California to dig for gold? California, too, was closer to Japan. He wanted to return home to his widowed mother of whom he had not heard since he last saw her back in 1841. He thought he could somehow make things easier for her by helping her make a living, if he returned. In the second place, he wanted to go back to Japan as soon as possible to tell his countrymen that Japan could no longer remain isolated from the rest of the world. He thought it urgent for his countrymen, who had much to catch up with, to open their eyes to the importance of learning modern science and adopting Western civilization. He was quite happy living with Captain Whitfield's family; he had good friends like Job Tripp. Most of the people of Fairhaven were kind to him. He thought he could get a permanent job as a seaman or a cooper and settle down in America without any trouble. But he felt it his duty to go back to Japan and do everything in his power to awaken the people before it was too late. However, he kept his plan to return to Japan a secret, thinking that Captain Whitfield would probably be greatly disappointed if he told him about it.

"I know if I should tell Captain and Mrs. Whitfield about my plan, they would probably never consent to it. They would think it too wild and too vague, and they would fear for my safety. I remember the captain once told me that I should certainly be put to death the moment I landed in Japan; no one is allowed to enter Japan from abroad. I remember Mrs. Whitfield once told me, 'You will make a good whaler like Captain Whitfield.' Yes, I might, if I try hard enough. Mr. Huzzy told me that I had the talent of a cooper. Perhaps I can be a successful cooper in New Bedford. But I always hear the voice of my old country calling me. I shall always be unhappy and lonely in my heart, if I don't see my mother once more, although I am happy now, living with Captain and Mrs. Whitfield, and I have many good friends here. I am sorry for my people; they know nothing about the rest of the world. Now is the time to let them know. I must return to help my countrymen open their eyes. I know it's a terrible thing to leave the house without telling the truth to Captain and Mrs. Whitfield, but they will understand some day. I'll only tell them that I am going to California to dig for gold. I shall never forget all my life their kindness and the good things they have taught me. Pardon me for my wickedness, but I must go."

In October, 1849, John Mung and a friend of his called Tilley started the long trip by working their passage on a lumber ship from New Bedford to California via Cape Horn. Not only was it the least expensive method of traveling, but it was also the safest way in those days when the overland journey by train was still in the future.

He and Tilley arrived in San Francisco toward the end of May of the following year. They stayed there for three days and were amazed at this booming town during the Gold Rush. Then they went to Sacramento in a paddle steamer.

John Mung had never sailed in a steamer before, although he had had an ample opportunity to observe steamers while in Fairhaven. Experienced seaman that he was, he was impressed by its speed and its ability to go in any direction irrespective of the wind and current. From Sacramento they took a train inland for a distance of about one hundred and twenty miles. Such a long train journey was also an eye-opening experience for Manjiro. He marveled at the great rapidity with which the objects by the side of the train sped away as the train went by. In all likelihood, Manjiro was the first Japanese national who ever experienced a journey by train and steamer.

At the foot of a mountain they got off the train, and on horseback and on foot they traveled over a dangerously steep path until at last they reached a gold mine. The weather was changeable here, very cold up in the mountain and very hot at its foot, and many people who had come to try their luck died. A mining town had come into existence almost overnight with mushrooming gambling houses and brothels crowded with gold diggers and outlaws.

Manjiro and his fellow worker Tilley went to the mining office and registered as gold miners. For it was the rule at that time that anyone who worked in this mine should sell all the gold or silver ore he had discovered to this office. Manjiro and his friend went to the North River mining lot and were employed by a certain contractor who lent them shovels, quarrying tools, tubs, basins, boxes and so forth. As it was already summer, it was unbearably hot inside the pit and many miners deserted this mine and went down the mountain to pan for gold in the river bed.

Manjiro and Tilley worked hard in this gold mine for about a month, at the end of which they had earned about one hundred and eighty pieces of silver. With this money they bought mining tools and started their gold digging in the river bed. They stayed at an inn which cost them as much as two dollars a day each, in spite of the fact that they ate nothing but pork and onions. They went to the river every day to find gold. On a lucky day, they found gold worth about twenty pieces of silver but when they were unlucky, they found absolutely nothing.

One day, just before sunset, Manjiro discovered a gold nugget almost as large as an egg. He did not know what to do, because it was too dangerous to take it with him to the inn where so many ruffians were waiting to take advantage of anyone who possessed plenty of gold. "Oh, yes, I have a good idea," whispered Manjiro to himself. "I'll bury it in the ground where I've found it and I'll stay right here until tomorrow morning." He did not breathe a word about the gold nugget even to Tilley. He simply said, "I'm not going back to the inn tonight." As soon as Tilley went away, he buried the gold nugget in the ground where he had found it, placed a large stone over the spot and sat on it all night. He went straightway to the office the first thing in the morning and exchanged it for money.

Thus they worked as gold diggers on their own and at the end of about two months Manjiro saved six hundred pieces of silver. He then decided to use the money for passage home. So he gave all his mining tools to Tilley, bade him farewell, and returned to San Francisco alone early in August.

In October, 1850, he embarked on a ship bound from San Francisco to Honolulu, intending to return to Japan with Denzo and his other three fellow countrymen from there. Again he worked his passage, because the ship's cap-

tain was very pleased to get the help of an experienced seaman like Manjiro. Upon his arrival in Honolulu, he went
to see Toraemon and sent for Denzo and his brother, who
were farming at Maeha. They all put their heads together
at once to discuss their passage back to Japan, but one thing
seemed to stand in their way. Goemon, brother of Denzo,
had been converted to the religion of the foreigners. Moreover, he had married a pretty native woman and was living
happily with her.

When Goemon heard about the plan to return to Japan,
he did not know what to do. It was not in him to leave his
beloved wife alone, perhaps never to see her again. But if he
lost this chance to go back now, he might lose it forever. As
to his foreign religion, he would be able to escape trouble
by keeping it a secret if questioned by Japanese officials. But
to bring a foreign woman into Japan was out of the question.
Denzo's heart was greatly troubled because he could not
decide what course his brother should take. It was as difficult to make his brother give up his good wife as it was to
leave him behind in the strange land. But Denzo himself
was firmly determined to take this opportunity of going
back.

They talked in Japanese, fearing the nature of their con-
versation might be known to others. Right or wrong, there
was an old saying in Tosa, "to make a devil of one's heart."
Denzo looked into his brother's face, but seeing it turn pale,
he said to John Mung, "Manjiro Nushi, listen! I have been
living all these years only to see my old country again."

John Mung nodded deeply but kept still until Goemon
broke the silence at last by saying, "I will go!"

HOMEWARD
BOUND

WHILE John Mung and his companions were discussing the plan to return home, word reached them by chance that a ship bearing several Japanese had arrived. John Mung at once ran to the harbor and visited the ship to meet them. But as their Japanese was entirely unintelligible to him, he sent for Denzo, who understood dialects. It was found that these newcomers from Japan were Torakichi and five other men of the *Tenju-maru*, a tangerine boat from Kishu, who had been rescued by an American ship when their boat was drifting at the mercy of a strong gale. Denzo and his friends had seen boats from Kishu, which often visited their native place. These newcomers also remembered the people of Tosa warmly and were very glad to learn that they might be able to return to Japan together.

Toraemon suddenly changed his mind and said that he would rather stay in Honolulu where he had many friends and that it did not make much difference whether he lived there or in Tosa. Greatly surprised, Denzo and John Mung tried all they could to persuade him to go with them. But Toraemon would not hear of such a thing. He said he was afraid that this attempt to return home would end in failure as it had before. After all, since he was doing very well as a cooper in Honolulu, he did not experience any homesickness that might otherwise have been growing in his heart.

The three men, though greatly disappointed with Toraemon, decided to leave him behind. They were to be allowed to sail in the ship that was to convey the rescued sailors of Kishu to Japan, but John Mung soon found that he was unable to put up with the captain of the ship. A few days before the ship was scheduled to sail, John Mung was mending a barrel on the deck since he had nothing to do then. Seeing John Mung at work, the captain came up to him and ordered that he mend all the broken barrels in the ship. "Aye, aye, sir," said John Mung and fell to work at once. When he had mended all the barrels, the captain brought all sorts of broken pieces of furniture and piled them high on the deck, saying, "You mend all these things. That's my order. Do you hear?" John Mung had some skill as a cooper, but as to furniture making and repairing he knew little.

"I'm sorry, sir," John Mung answered, "I can't repair all those things." The captain, without saying so much as a word, slapped him on the cheek. The act, which might have been reserved for a slave, enraged him.

"I am not your slave," declared John Mung. "You are putting on airs with that clay pipe sticking out of your mouth. Don't you know how to behave like an honorable seaman?"

Uttering a curse, he refused point-blank to repair the broken chairs and tables before him. Greatly annoyed, the captain tried to frighten him into obedience, but he looked the captain in the face and held his own. "I'm not sailing with you in this ship," said Manjiro defiantly. He decided to put off going back until another opportunity presented itself, and he and Goemon and Denzo, much disappointed, left the ship. Torakichi and the other Kishu sailors, knowing how heartbreaking it was for the three men, said simply, "We're sorry for you."

John Mung and the two brothers went straightway to see Toraemon, the cooper, who laughed at them as much as to say, "It served you right." But suddenly, knitting his brows, he told them that there was some difficulty.

Every day, for four or five successive days, Goemon's wife had come to see him demanding, "Where is Goemon? Tora Nushi, you know where he is." Toraemon had simply said, "I don't know." Although she was such a good, gentle woman, there'd be much trouble this time. Goemon had slipped out of his house without letting his wife know anything about his plan. Word that their attempt to go back to Japan had failed again would surely be rumored all over Honolulu. Even worse, it might be reported in the *Polynesian* and the *Friend* which were two rival newspapers in Hawaii always trying to beat each other with such stories.

When Denzo and Goemon returned to their house in Maeha, ten miles from Honolulu, they found Goemon's wife kneeling before a picture of Christ and praying a fervent prayer. At the sound of footsteps she jumped up and seeing Goemon standing there, she flung herself upon him with a cry and clung fast to his shoulders. Overwhelmed by joy, she wept with her face pressed on his breast and then she kissed him again and again. Denzo had been quite accustomed to see her kiss her husband, but this time he found it more than he could stand. So he left them alone and quickly went out to work in the field, taking a hoe from the dirt floor of the cottage.

John Mung was waiting for a chance to go back to Japan by working his passage. He had asked some of his friends in town whether or not it was possible to find a suitable ship for him. One day, he heard the news that a certain ship was ready to sail for China. It was an American merchant ship, the *Sarah Boyd*, which entered Honolulu late in November, 1850, and was sailing for China to pick up a cargo of China tea. John Mung brought this good news to Denzo and his brother, and at once they all went to see Captain Whitmore of the *Sarah Boyd*.

When John Mung told the captain their story and asked his permission to sail in the ship, the captain refused, saying, "I know very well how you wish to return to your old country. But I am sorry to say that the ship that goes to Shanghai to take on a cargo passes far south of Japan. Besides, a merchant ship, unlike a whaling boat, must run her course according to a schedule. It is out of the question to change her course in order to touch at a Japanese port. You see, the *Sarah Boyd* belongs to a shipping company and it is essential, therefore, to deliver her cargo of tea within a fixed time to the merchants for whom no delivery is too early. At any rate, I can't act on my own authority as to changing her course."

In spite of these words, Captain Whitmore was touched by their passionate desire to go home. So he spread a chart before them and explained.

"You see, this is the China Sea. This is Satsuma of Japan. The ship sometimes passes through the waters of Satsuma in a fair wind. If that's the case, landing on one of those islands near Satsuma might be possible. It all depends upon a favorable wind."

John Mung, Denzo and Goemon began talking the matter over among themselves. They might be taken to Shanghai and back to Honolulu, were the wind unfavorable. Yet if they lost this chance, they might never have another one. Sail they must in this ship, come what may. They put their heads together to discuss how they should enter their native country whose doors were so tightly closed. At last John Mung hit upon a happy plan when all the others failed. According to his plan, he would buy a small boat to be carried on the *Sarah Boyd,* and when she entered the waters of Japan, the boat would be lowered to reach the land. Denzo and Goemon thought it a splendid idea and at once seconded it. Captain Whitmore, also thinking that the plan might work, said, "How clever you are, John Mung!" And he nodded approvingly.

Leaving the *Sarah Boyd,* the three men went straight to see Toraemon and tried to talk him into joining in their scheme. But Toraemon would not listen to such a proposal, on the ground that crossing the sea in a small boat was too dangerous. Evidently he had given up the hope of ever going back to Japan.

John Mung proceeded to the U.S. consulate in Honolulu and thanked the American authorities there for the kindness shown him and his friends. Mr. Elisha H. Allen, U.S. consul, wrote a letter introducing them and asking all those who might come into contact with them to treat them kindly. He also mentioned in the letter about the desire of the American people to establish good relations with Japan even before Commodore Perry came to Japan.

Consulate of the United States,
   Honolulu, Hawaiian Islands

To all whom these presents shall, doth or may come; I, Elisha H. Allen, Consul of the United States of America, Hawaiian Islands, send greetings:

Know ye, that satisfactory evidence has been produced to me that John Manjiro, Denzo, and Goemon left the southwest part of the Island of Nippon, Japan, in a fishing vessel and were wrecked; and after remaining on an uninhabited island for about six months they were taken off by Captain Whitfield of the American whaleship *John Howland*, who brought them to the Sandwich Islands. Denzo and Goemon remained here; Manjiro went cruising for whales, and in the year of eighteen hundred and forty-four reached the United States of America. He remained there two years, spending his time in farming, learning the cooper's trade and attending school. He went on another voyage sperm whaling, and returned to the United States in the year of eighteen hundred and forty-nine. Last October he arrived here again, after having visited California, the gold region of the United States of America.

Captain Whitmore has kindly consented to take them in the bark *Sarah Boyd*, a vessel belonging to the United States of America, and leave them near the Loochoo Islands. Some friends here aided them in making preparations for their voyage and I trust they will be kindly treated by all they may meet.

I am informed by the Captain of the Seaman's Friend Society, that John Manjiro has sustained a good character and has improved in knowledge. He will tell his countrymen of Japan how happy the Americans would be to make their acquaintance, and visit them with their ships, and give gold and silver for their goods.

Given under my hand and the seal of this Consulate at Honolulu this thirteenth day of December in the year of our Lord Eighteen Hundred and Fifty.

ELISHA H. ALLEN
U. S. Consul

John Mung got busy going around visiting people and trying to buy a small boat which was necessary for their voyage. He had some money and gold dust which he had found in California. But as a newly launched boat was too expensive, he tried to buy a second-hand one that was still seaworthy. Fortunately, he heard the news that a certain Englishman was willing to part with a second-hand boat which was apparently in good condition. So he went and bought it with complete equipment for a hundred and twenty-five dollars.

John Mung christened this boat the *Adventure* and took it on board the *Sarah Boyd*. Some of the people of Honolulu, hearing about this brave adventure, came to help them with the preparations for sailing. The Reverend Samuel C. Damon, appealing to the public in the newspaper *Polynesian* to contribute money for their benefit, raised funds for them from many citizens of Honolulu. The *Polynesian* printed the following article written by the Reverend S. C. Damon on November 14, 1850:

Expedition for Japan. The public is aware that from time to time wrecked Japanese have been brought to the Sandwich Islands. There are now three who were brought hither by Captain W. H. Whitfield in 1841. One of them, John Manjiro, accompanied Captain Whitfield to the United States, where he was educated in a good common school, besides having acquired the cooper's trade.

He has returned to the islands, and here finds his former shipmates, two of whom propose to accompany him, and if possible, return to Japan. He has purchased a good whaleboat and outfit; Captain Whitmore of the American ship *Sarah Boyd*, bound from Mazatlan, Mexico, to Shanghai, China, having kindly consented to leave them somewhere off the Loochoo Islands and from thence they hope to make their way to Japan.

To complete the outfit is wanted — a compass, a good fowl-ing-piece, a few articles of clothing, shoes, and a nautical almanac for 1850. Will not some benevolent person aid forward the enterprise? The subscriber will be responsible for the safe delivery of the articles referred to.

S. C. DAMON

From this article in the newspaper, Goemon's wife learned, to her great sorrow, that her husband again was secretly planning to return to Japan. But she knew already that her husband had irretrievably made up his mind to return home and she could do nothing about it. She managed to be resigned to her fate.

John Mung wrote to his benefactor, Captain Whitfield, thanking him deeply for his great kindness of the past many years, and deeply apologizing for his act of ingratitude in leaving him for good without saying goodbye to him. He asked the captain to give away his possessions he had left in the house to his friends back in Fairhaven.

Goemon and Denzo went to see their friends in Honolulu to say goodbye. But as the ship was setting sail sooner than expected, the farewell calls had to be done in a hurry and they went on board the ship a little lonely and sad, although they were going home at last.

A HAPPY
LANDFALL

THE *Sarah Boyd,* measuring a hundred and twenty feet in length, and carrying a crew of seventeen, left Oahu on December 17, but as she soon met bad weather she lost her normal speed considerably. When the ship reached a point four miles from Ryukyu on January 2, according to the Japanese calendar, after almost seventy long days of sailing, John Mung and the other two were overwhelmed with the joy of returning home at last. He wrote at once to his friends in Oahu telling them of this great joy and asked them to tell Toraemon to come to share it, sending the letter through the kindness of Captain Whitmore.

"That direction," said Captain Whitmore, pointing toward the island in the distance, "may hide death in store for you, I am afraid, for your country strictly bars out anyone from abroad. Why don't you give up the whole idea of going back to your country and instead go to China with us and return to Honolulu in this ship?"

"How can I do such a thing? If I don't take this chance, I may never see my mother. Besides, I must return to my countrymen at once and tell them that they must open their eyes before it is too late. They cannot remain isolated from the rest of the world forever," answered Manjiro, firmly determined to run any risk. "Thank you for your advice but my mind is made up." The captain still looked as if he could not understand John Mung at all and said, "All right, but remember, if you run into trouble, you have nobody but yourself to blame."

At last the captain ordered his men to stop the ship and had the *Adventure* lowered on the rough sea. He shook hands with each of the Japanese just before they went into the boat and said, "This is a risky landing, my friends. The sea is rather choppy today. Come back to the ship if you fail to reach the shore. Don't take chances, understand? The law of your country to keep out foreigners is so strict that I'm afraid I shall never see you again. Now let me wish all of you and the *Adventure* the best of luck!"

"Thank you, sir, for all you have done for us," said John Mung. "But the time will come, Captain, sooner or later when your ship will freely enter Japanese ports."

Captain Whitmore smiled and simply said, "Who knows?" The three men exchanged words of farewell with the sailors and thanked them for everything. Then they went into the boat and began to pull it over the tossing waves toward the island. The men of the *Sarah Boyd* kept watching the boat for a long time, waving their hands. When they saw it safely approach the island, they started the ship under full sail and soon went out of sight beyond the western horizon.

The three men directed the boat close to the rocky shore, but a heavy wind and rain began to rage and prevented them from landing. It was dark already. So they decided to spend that night under the lee of the cliff and wait for the dawn. The boat was heavily loaded with food, their personal effects, and presents, but it was so strongly built that it could easily stand the stormy sea.

The wind and rain ceased with the dawn of January 3. The houses with orange gardens came in sight beyond the beach to which the three men rowed the boat. Denzo went ashore first to take in the general situation. As he had retained his Japanese language better than anyone else, he went to one of the houses and asked the name of the place, but the people in that house were scandalized at the sight of a man in foreign clothes, and their peaceful New Year family breakfast ended in bedlam.

Uttering some outlandish words, they raised a hue and cry and ran out of the house. Denzo tried to explain that he was a harmless fellow, but his Tosa dialect was no more intelligible to the natives than their speech was to him. Running away from those excited people, he went back to the boat and reported what had happened. "They don't understand me," said Denzo. "I'm afraid I've forgotten Japanese. I've been away so long."

John Mung fastened the boat to the shore, and with a pistol in his pocket, he headed toward the straggling houses, Denzo and Goemon following. He met a native on the road, but his word being unintelligible, he imitated a man who drank water out of his hands until the native led them to a well. They fetched their kitchen tools from the boat and cooked beef and pork, for they had not eaten anything since the night before. To crown the joy of the feast, they drank coffee. As they were taking an after-dinner rest, a group of natives came, and thinking that these three men were stranded foreigners, took them to a cottage which seemed to be a watchman's lodge.

The islanders treated them kindly, giving them drinking water, potatoes, and rice. In the meantime, a village official who had been sent for and who was accompanied by some village clerks arrived to investigate the matter.

The official questioned the men as to their nationality, their names, the port of embarkation, the port of debarkation, and their possessions. He disarmed John Mung and told them that they would be sent to the Village Office for further examination. The place where they landed was a village called Mabunimagiri in the southern extreme of Okinawa Island, Ryukyu.

John Mung and the others were taken to a village called Nakao where the Village Office was located, escorted by more than ten armed officials who never took their eyes off them. Denzo who had trouble with his eyes was allowed to ride in a litter. Although the three men were not treated harshly by any means, they were closely watched by the escorting officials who thought they might be foreigners after all.

The two villages, Mabunimagiri and Nakao, were connected by a road four miles long. On arriving at Nakao, the three men were first sent to the house of a farmer called Peichin. That night they were summoned to the Village Office to be cross-questioned till a late hour. But they could not understand each other very well, so the investigation was adjourned till the next morning. The investigation convinced the officials that they were of Japanese nationality. Peichin, too, in whose house the three men were staying, testified that the stranded men were Japanese as he had seen them eat rice with chopsticks. But as to whether they were dangerous characters or civilized people even the officials apparently found it hard to tell.

It was on January 14 when the days of New Year jubilation were over, that John Mung and the others were again summoned to the Village Office, where a senior official and three lower officials from Satsuma carefully examined their personal effects and books. The books were examined page by page with special attention and curiosity. The topographical survey textbook must have struck them as suspicious, for the official's eyes were riveted on the enigmatic symbols in it, while the three menial officials, whose eyes also pored over those illustrations, thought it no more than a book of nonsense. They whispered to themselves that those circles made with a pair of compasses were like playful pictures drawn on the ground by foreign children. Then the senior official from Satsuma said admonishingly, "No! These must be symbols used in some profound learning."

The senior official from Satsuma, whose name was Shonoshin Ogawa, was a good-natured young samurai. He told the village officials to be kind and helpful to the castaways, and advised John Mung not to let rashness get the better of him under any circumstances. He told about a fisherman of Sendai called Sajuro who had returned from Russia where he had been rescued in a shipwreck, and how he had killed himself, unable to stand the harshness of his trial. The official from Satsuma assured John Mung that the Lord of Satsuma would always treat stranded men with mercy. The severe questioning to which John Mung and the others had been put, before they were turned over to the Governor of Nagasaki under the Tokugawa Government, was in accordance with the law — a matter of formality after all. John Mung and the others felt relieved by this and thanked him for his kind advice. Of course, they had never dreamed of the popular outcry, "Down with the Tokugawa Government," which was increasingly making itself heard in Satsuma.

They were still detained in the house of Peichin as ordered by the senior Satsuma official and were constantly watched by two of the five Satsuma officials and two Ryukyu officials by turns. But as to their treatment there was nothing left to be desired. Their food was paid for by the local government. Peichin served his guests liberally at every meal with various kinds of delicious food such as pork, chicken, fish and eggs, while occasionally Ryukyu whisky was among the gifts from the lord. As to their clothes, Japanese *haori* and *hakama* were given by the chief of Ryukyu, and as it was soon summer, mosquito nets, summer kimonos, and underwear were also given to them. This kind of life lasted seven months and finally it was decided that John Mung and the others should be taken to Satsuma on July 18. Guarded by the officials again, the three men, carried in litters, left Peichin's house in the evening with their American articles borne by some natives. Peichin walked with them to the village border to bid them farewell. As it was quite dark, they could not get a roadside view of the country. No sooner had they arrived in Naha, capital of Ryukyu, than they were taken to a ship which was ready to set sail. The port of Naha and its neighborhood were hidden in darkness from their observation.

The ship cast anchor just outside the port of Yamakawa,

Satsuma, on the evening of July 29. Two boats were put
out from the ship to carry them to Kagoshima before the
dawn of the thirtieth. They were taken in or out of the ship
always under cover of darkness, which prevented them from
observing the ports. As soon as they landed, they were taken
into custody at Nishidamachi, Kagoshima, guarded by some
petty samurai. Satsuma was a great feudal province, and
the guards showed the utmost politeness to the men as the
Lord of Satsuma privately desired. They were served with
all sorts of delicacies of land and sea and with wine as fine
as ever they drank. The lord granted them gifts of the
summer kimonos, underwear and hemp garments and even
the winter *haori* and the cotton padded kimono which they
did not need as yet.

The trial of the castaways lasted for several days under
an official who would leave no stone unturned to find out
what he could. One day, Lord Nariaki himself summoned
the three men. After feasting them, he sat with them alone
in order to ask them all sorts of questions about America.
The three men had already shaven the temples of their
heads according to the Japanese custom. They were dressed
in kimonos, and that day they put on the *hakama* which
were the gifts from the lord to be received in audience.
The lord summoned them not merely because he was interested in examining their foreign articles and clothes but
because he wanted to get as much information as possible
about the political, educational and military conditions in
America. He also asked them about American manners,
fashions, and customs concerning weddings and funerals.
Denzo and Goemon, nervous and shy in the presence of the
lord, felt tongue-tied, but John Mung boldly told the lord
how highly civilized and progressive America was, citing

all sorts of examples. The lord listened intently to John Mung's talk, nodding a little from time to time. But when John Mung said that in America the value of a man was judged according to his ability, the lord nodded a great nod.

The trial was held every day for forty-eight days, at the end of which a report from the lord to the Tokugawa Government was at last written to this effect:

Mabunimagiri of Ryukyu: three strange-looking men in a boat were drifted ashore on January 3. Our officials who had been sent there to examine them, found that they were Denzo and his brother Goemon of Usaura, Takaoka-gun, Tosa, and Manjiro of Nakanohama. Those three and Jusuke, brother of Denzo, and Toraemon of Usaura put to sea for fishing in January of the Year of the Cow and had met a storm which sent them to a lonely island in the direction of the Dragon. They lived chiefly on bird meat until June 27 when a foreign ship passed by the island. Approaching at their signal, the ship was found to be an American whaling ship. They asked for help and were taken onto the ship which in October reached Oahu. They were placed under the care of the captain's friends there, except Manjiro who was told he would be taken to the mainland. Sailing in November, the ship reached America in April of the next year. After a few years there, Manjiro left and came back to Oahu, where he and his friends earned their living until they heard about a ship bound for China. Their request to be conveyed on board the ship to Japan was refused, the passage to Japan being closed as yet. Whereupon, they said they would sail in a ship with a small boat, which they would purchase, and when Japan was sighted, they would ask permission to lower the boat. Jusuke had been dead these five years and Toraemon was left behind as that was his own wish. Leaving the port in December, the ship came to where Ryukyu was in sight and the boat was pushed off. The wind and waves were too rough to land, so staying overnight behind a cliff, they landed the following day, while the ship sailed away toward the west according to their statement. If they had been brought to the shore by the ship, we could have prohibited them from landing. But we could do nothing about it since they came ashore in a boat in which no foreigner came with them. They were again put to examination which proved again that they were quite innocent of the evil foreign religion or other crimes. So we have decided to keep them under protection until we hand them over to the Governor of Nagasaki.

HOME
AT LAST

THE THREE MEN, accompanied by the officials, left Kagoshima on September 16, 1851, and reached the port of
Kyodomari two days later, whence they embarked on a
transport again under cover of darkness. This ship had
thirteen sails and eight oars and on its deck was built a
pavilion showing a family crest of a bridle. The ship mark
of the feudal Satsuma clan was hoisted at its bow. The
party arrived safely at Nagasaki on the twenty-ninth of the
same month.

On October 1, John Mung and the two other Japanese
were taken ashore and sent to the Office of Nagasaki, where
they were examined by Governor Maki Shima while their
statements were minutely recorded in a book, *The Narratives of the Castaways*. The trials were held eighteen times

but what they said was the repetition of what they had
already told at Satsuma. Again they related their experiences abroad, the names of the countries they had visited,
the customs and manners, food, industries, farm products,
geography, flora, ceremonies, politics and military conditions of those countries.

John Mung's observations recorded in *The Narratives of
the Castaways,* unlike those of other castaways, are generally correct and to the point. Speaking of the politics
and finance of Hawaii he says:

Honolulu, which is the capital of Hawaii, is on Oahu and
has become very prosperous in recent years as ships from all
parts of the world enter this port. The wealth of the seven
islands is estimated at one hundred and twenty thousand silver
coins, of which sixty thousand belongs to King Kamehameha
while the other sixty thousand belongs to the governor from
America who owns half of the land. If America tries to take
possession of these islands, Britain would protest and if Britain
tries to do the same, Spain would likewise protest. Though
a small country, it belongs to none of them and, therefore, the
ship mark of this country is a combination of the marks of
these three countries. All the seven islands are rather moun-
tainous, but a few sandy places on them are good enough for
the cultivation of potatoes or onions. It is said one hundred
and twenty thousand silver coins are raised every year by taxes,
mainly those levied on ships entering the port.

Then in referring to the government of America he says
something like this:

Having been founded by Englishmen, the country is full of
them. They are white-complexioned and the color of their
eyes is a little yellow. As there is no hereditary king in this

country, a man of great knowledge and ability is elected king who holds his office for four years and then he is succeeded by another. When the administration is good under a certain king and his popularity continues, he sits on the throne for another four years. He lives a very simple life and goes out on horseback accompanied by one servant. Officials there are not haughty; indeed, it is hard to tell them from ordinary citizens. The present king is called Taylor, an Englishman by blood, who, during the war with Mexico which was fought over the border question, led his army to a great victory which won for him so great a fame that at last he was made king. This year being the Year of the Rat, another king is to succeed the present one.

As to the criminal law, he says:

The prisoners have certain freedoms within an enclosure and they are made to do something in their line, such as making cloth or various other articles. The term of imprisonment is determined by the gravity of a crime. A murderer is usually punished with death. When he is to be executed, a scaffold is raised on which he is made to stand with a noose around his neck, and upon the reading of the death sentence the trap-door upon which he is standing opens, causing him to fall, to be hanged by the neck. However, I have not seen an execution myself.

John Mung had no knowledge of Commodore Perry's plan to visit Japan which was to be executed in 1853. However, he refers to the general situation which made Perry's expedition necessary.

Seven years ago, a warship from a port called Boston went on a cruise visiting various countries for a survey. Upon entering a port of Japan to get water and fuel, this warship, I hear, was ordered to leave at once and was compelled to do so without accomplishing its purpose. When a survey ship or a whaleship runs into a storm, it often runs short of fresh water and fuel, and the captain of the ship asks the local authorities at the nearest port for permission to take on fresh supplies, even offering a hostage, if necessary. But the Japanese authorities make a great fuss on such an occasion and flatly refuse to comply with the reasonable request, to the great discomfort of the captain and crew. Such stories have often been reported in detail in newspapers. Generally speaking, the Japanese are quick-tempered, while the people over there are broad-minded, and as their country is now being opened, they have no design to take land from any other country. American ships have entered the port of Nagasaki three times, pretending to be English or Dutch, but each time they have been found out and forced to leave the port. In sailing to China from California, a ship carries many passengers as well as its cargo and, therefore, it cannot be loaded with enough coal. The distance between America and China being a matter of fourteen or fifteen hundred *ri*, it is almost impossible for the ship to make a long voyage back to California to get coal when it has run short of it. So I understand, they desire to have a coaling station in Satsuma, Nippon. I happened to read this story when I was in Oahu last year.

At the end of the trial the men were put to the usual test of stamping on the picture of Christ. John Mung often attended the Sunday services in Fairhaven, and as Goemon was a servant to a Honolulu missionary, he used to hear Christian sermons and say Christian prayers. But they knew nothing about the bronze tablet of the crucifix, so they stamped on it nonchalantly, only to please the inquisitorial official.

"Tell me, how did you feel when you stamped on the tablet?" asked the official.

"I felt rather cold," replied John Mung whose feet had been so accustomed to the foreign shoes which he had been wearing for so many years that he must have felt particularly cold when his feet touched the bronze tablet.

When the investigation was over, they were again put into custody at a feudal town called Sakura-machi, whereupon John Mung was enraged and became rebellious when he was put into prison instead of being released at once as he had expected. Denzo, seeing John Mung lose his temper, advised him in English, "Take it easy! Take it easy! Mr. John Mung."

In the dark prison house, there were several other prisoners and while John Mung and the two others were huddling together in one dark corner someone accosted them unexpectedly.

"If it is not Den Nushi! . . ."

"If it is not Manjiro Nushi!"

It was Torakichi and the four others of the *Tenju-maru* of Hidaka, Kishu, the men whom John Mung and the others had met in Honolulu. According to Torakichi, he and his party were taken to China from Honolulu by an American ship and then returned to Nagasaki by a Chinese ship, to be sentenced to only three days' imprisonment according to the law.

The men from Kishu thought that the imprisonment was rather a matter of formality and, indeed, they received kind treatment, except for the fact that they were not allowed to go out. In the evening, the *Joruri* tellers (a kind of Japanese ballad singers) often came to entertain them by reciting the romance of *Osome-Hisamatsu* and other famous tales. John Mung was much impressed by the words of romance in those tales and realized the beauty of the language for the first time in his life.

Both the Kishu and Tosa parties were released from the prison at last and the three men belonging to the Tosa party were sent to the house of Sanjiro Nishikawa, purveyor to the Tosa clan. Those articles which they brought from America were returned to them, except a barometer, an octant, seventeen English books, gold dust, gold coins, silver coins, a musket with a bayonet, two pistols, shot and foreign dice, which were all confiscated by the officials. The *Adventure*, which had cost them one hundred and twenty-five dollars, also had to be given up. Thus the trial of the castaways having been completed at last, they stayed on with Sanjiro Nishikawa waiting for the arrival of the officials from Tosa who were coming to take them home. In the meantime, the Kochi clan of Tosa received the following letter in October:

We notify you that Denzo, Goemon and Manjiro of Usaura, Takaoka-gun, in the Province of Tosa, who had been rescued by a foreign whaling ship and landed in Ryukyu, were handed over to us by Governor Matsudaira of Satsuma. We request that you send your officials to the Nagasaki Office where we intend to commit the repatriates to your authority.

On receipt of this letter, the Tosa clan decided to let Sasuke Horibe proceed to Nagasaki to receive the three men and bring them to Tosa. Horibe, accompanied by several officials, left Kochi by sea in early June, 1852, reaching Nagasaki in the middle of June. Just before the party of Manjiro left Nagasaki, the Governor of Nagasaki issued the following statement:

I do hereby certify that Denzo, his younger brother Goemon of Usaura, Takaoka-gun, in the Province of Tosa, territory of

Lord Matsudaira of Tosa, and Manjiro of Nakanohama, Harita-gun, in the same province, were stranded on a desert island in the Year of the Cow, were rescued by an American ship, lived in foreign parts for several years, returned to Ryukyu, and upon examination at this office of their lives abroad, they proved to be innocent of being converted to Christianity and other evil faiths; in short, they are fit to be returned to their native province.

It is imperative, however, that they should not live here-after outside the said province and that we should be duly noti-fied in case of their death.

Articles acquired or purchased abroad, such as gold dust, coins, gold, silver and copper, guns, bullets, drugs, an octant, foreign dice and also the boat and its tackle shall be confis-cated. Japanese silver pieces shall be granted in exchange for the gold dust and foreign coins.

Those confiscated articles as listed in the above letter were mostly John Mung's property, for Denzo and Goemon had taken no chance and had conformed to the law ban-ning the articles of foreign countries.

The three men, accompanied by Sasuke Horibe and his party, sailed from Nagasaki on June 25, 1852, a year and a half after their landing in Ryukyu, and entered Urado on June 30. They were made to stay at an inn of Urado and were summoned to the Office there every day to be ex-amined again, despite the written statement proving their innocence issued by the Office of Nagasaki. Manjiro and the other repatriates repeated what they had told the offi-cials of Nagasaki about their experience abroad.

They told the officials of Tosa what they had told the officials of Ryukyu, Satsuma and Nagasaki. Manjiro had been held in Ryukyu for six months, at Satsuma for two

months and at Nagasaki for ten months, chiefly for investigation. It was more than he could stand. Naturally he grew
impatient when he knew that he was about to be put to
another long session of interrogation in the very province
where his family, all his relatives and friends were eagerly
waiting for his return.

"What is the meaning of all this?" Manjiro demanded.
"I told them everything already."

"That may be so but you haven't told us anything yet,"
said the official. As was the case with other clans, the
Tosa clan wanted to learn firsthand from Manjiro as much
as possible about foreign countries. Far from regarding
Manjiro and the others as outlaws, the officials treated them
most hospitably, giving them good food and fine clothes.
On September 24, Manjiro was asked to appear before the
members of the family of the Daimyo of Tosa in a suit of
foreign clothes just to show what it looked like.

The investigation being over, Manjiro left Kochi on the
early morning of October 1, with Denzo and his brother,
and reached Usaura on the evening of the same day. They
found that Denzo's family had ceased to exist and that not
a trace of his former house was to be seen, so Denzo and
his brother went to one of their relatives to live temporarily.

Leaving Usaura on the morning of October 2, Manjiro
set out on foot on the last leg of the long journey which
stretched seventy miles through the familiar countryside.
He spent three nights at roadside farmhouses and reached
Nakanohama at last on the afternoon of October 5.

Word had already reached the village that Manjiro was
coming, and his family, relatives and almost all the villagers
were on hand to welcome him at the village headman's.
When they met Manjiro, however, for the first time in

twelve years, they could hardly believe their eyes. The Manjiro in front of them, elegantly dressed in his formal *hakama* and *haori*, looking much more dignified and intelligent than the village squire, was quite different from the poor fisherman's boy they remembered so well.

"Mother, here I am at last!" said Manjiro.

"Is that really you, my son?" said his mother as though she were unable to believe that the fine young man in front of her was her own son.

"Yes, I am indeed your son."

They both stood there for a while unable to speak. Then Manjiro took his mother in his arms and they both cried. Many villagers cried, too.

"Is it possible," one of them said in a whisper, "that that poor fisherman's boy could have become such a gentleman?"

"I really don't understand," said another.

"It's so good to see you again," said Manjiro to the villagers; "this is certainly the happiest day in my life! I thank you for every kindness you have shown my family while I have been away."

Then Manjiro accompanied by his family and friends went to the village graveyard and "reported" his return home to his father. While he offered a prayer of thanks, the smoke rising from the burning incense offered to the spirit of the father filled the air of the early Autumn, and suddenly he remembered Fairhaven and Captain Whitfield.

That night there was a great rejoicing and feast in the house to which his relatives and friends came. When Manjiro told his story about foreign countries and how he had lived among foreigners, they all listened in amazement. But when the talk was over, someone asked him, "Do they have thunderstorms and the four seasons in America?"

Another, "How is it possible to live without rice?" Manjiro answered those questions in detail although he thought them silly. They are simple people, after all, said Manjiro to himself. At any rate, when Manjiro sipped *sake* and ate a broiled red sea bream fresh from the sea of Tosa and boiled rice and red beans prepared by his mother, he knew he had returned home at last.

But the happy reunion was abruptly brought to an end when it was only three days old. A messenger came from the Daimyo of Tosa telling him that it was the wish of the lord that he should become an official instructor at the school of the Tosa clan in Kochi. Much as he regretted leaving Nakanohama, of which he had dreamed so often when he was roaming up and down the world, he decided to accede to the wish of his feudal lord. Besides, he gladly thought that the opportunity to teach his countrymen the ways of civilization and to let them know that it was no time for Japan to keep her doors closed to the rest of the world had presented itself unexpectedly. He found in the Kyojukan School in Kochi a class of students hungry for knowledge about foreign countries, to whom he taught various subjects of science as well as English.

He knew that he was constantly watched by "too many eyes" and that he had to use great discretion in the class. He did not say in so many words publicly that Japan should open the country to foreigners, but he did not hesitate for a moment to teach them the facts about the civilized world, so that the students could decide for themselves unmistakably what was to be done about the future of their country:

"I remember when I told an official who investigated me at Kagoshima that the American horse was bigger and stronger than the Japanese horse, he got very angry, thinking perhaps I was telling a lie at the expense of our country. There are many countrymen who believe that I don't hold my own country in respect, if I tell them that America and other Western nations are more advanced in science than Japan. But it is a fact. I'd rather not say definitely that Japan should open its doors to foreigners at once. Perhaps, it is better to do a thing gradually. But whether we like it or not, the day will come when Japan must put an end to its closed-door policy; because only then can we build our country into a modern nation. When that day comes, the opportunity for you young men will be limitless and a bright future will surely dawn upon our country."

In recognition of the service rendered by Manjiro as an instructor, the Daimyo of Tosa presented him with a sword, granting him the privilege of wearing it at his waist. But Manjiro, having lived many years in America, distrusted the samurai's side arms. He often tied the sword with a Japanese towel and carried it about as if it were a nuisance.

"I have no use for a sword in time of peace," he would say to anyone who asked him why he did such a strange thing.

Manjiro had already told the Daimyo of Satsuma and other Japanese officials who investigated him about some of the enlightening facts concerning America and its people. Almost everything he said was a revelation to those who had for centuries been living in insular isolation. Never did he hesitate to point out to them that America was not a country of "foreign barbarians," as some people believed, but, on the contrary, much more advanced in many ways than Japan. The influence of his revelations had been limited to the local clans with which he had come into contact, but

when he was invited by the Tokugawa Government, soon
after Commodore Perry and his fleet appeared in the Bay
of Uraga in 1853, he had a vital role to play for the wakening
of the Japanese people to world civilization. Upon his arrival in Yedo, the former capital of Japan, he was examined
by Magistrate Saemon Kawaji before he was officially taken
into government service.

Answering the questions put to him by the investigating
official, he revealed his own observations about America to
the amazement of his listeners. Never can we overestimate
the value of these observations which undoubtedly in-
fluenced the policy of the Tokugawa Government in favor
of the opening of the country to foreign intercourse when
Commodore Perry revisited Japan in February, 1854. They
were recorded in a report made by the investigator. Touching upon the geography, people and products of America,
he is quoted as saying:

The United States of America occupies the vast area of
North America extending from about 30 degrees to approxi-
mately 50 degrees [N.L.]. The west coast faces Europe across
the seas, large and small; the south borders on Mexico. The
North and South Americas are separated by the Gulf. The
northern borders abut on the various countries belonging to
England. The United States of America, which has thirty-
eight states now, has pushed forward its borders and has become a powerful nation. The country is generally blessed with
a mild climate and it is rich in natural resources such as gold,
silver, copper, iron, timber and other materials that are necessary for man's living. The land, being fertile, yields abundant
crops of wheat, barley, corn, beans and all sorts of vegetables,
but rice is not grown there simply because they do not eat it.

While I was in California, large quantities of gold and silver were discovered. People flocked to the gold mines from all parts of the world, even from China. I saw some people who had made fortunes from their gold mines riding in carriages having silver wheels and I also saw they were using many gold or silver wares.

Both men and women are generally good-looking but as they came from different countries of Europe, their features and the color of their eyes, hair and skin are not the same. They are usually tall in stature. They are by nature sturdy, vigorous, capable and warmhearted people. American women have quaint customs; for instance, some of them make a hole through the lobes of their ears and run a gold or silver ring through this hole as an ornament.

Then Manjiro went on to tell the officials about the strange customs of the Americans:

When a young man wants to marry, he looks for a young woman for himself, without asking a go-between to find one for him, as we do in Japan, and, if he succeeds in finding a suitable one, he asks her whether or not she is willing to marry him. If she says, "Yes," he tells her and his parents about it and then the young man and the young woman accompanied by their parents and friends go to church and ask the priest to perform the wedding ceremony. Then the priest asks the bridegroom, "Do you really want to have this young woman as your wife?" To which the young man says, "I do". Then the priest asks a similar question of the bride and when she says, "I do," he declares that they are man and wife. Afterward, cakes and refreshments are served and then the young man takes his bride on a pleasure trip.

Both American men and women make love openly and appear wanton by nature, but they are unexpectedly strict about their relations. Husband and wife have great attachment for each other and their home life is very affectionate. No other nation can be a match for the Americans in this respect.

Refined Americans generally do not touch liquor. Even if they do so they drink only a little, because they think that liquor makes men either lazy or quarrelsome. Vulgar Americans, however, drink just like Japanese, although drunkards are detested and despised. Even the whalers, who are hard drinkers while they are on a voyage, stop drinking once they are on shore. Moreover, the quality of liquor is inferior to Japanese *sake*, in spite of the fact that there are many kinds of liquor in America.

Americans invite a guest to a dinner at which fish, fowl and cakes are served, but to the best of my knowledge, a guest, however important he may be, is served with no liquor at all. He is often entertained with music instead when the dinner is over.

When a visitor enters the house he takes off his hat. They never bow to each other as politely as we do. The master of the house simply stretches out his right hand and the visitor also does the same and they shake hands with each other. While they exchange greetings, the master of the house invites the visitor to sit on a chair instead of the floor. As soon as business is over, the visitor takes leave of the house, because they do not want to waste time.

When a mother happens to have very little milk in her breasts to give her child, she gives of all things a cow's milk, as a substitute for a mother's milk. But it is true that no ill effect of this strange habit has been reported from any part of the country.

On every seventh day, people, high and low, stop their work and go to temple and keep their houses quiet, but on the other days they take pleasure by going into mountains and fields to hunt, while lower class Americans take their women to the seaside or hills and drink and bet and have a good time.

The temple is called church. The priest, who is an ordinary-looking man, has a wife and he even eats meat, unlike a Japanese priest. Even on the days of abstinence, he only refrains from eating animal meat and he does not hesitate to eat fowl or fish instead. The church is a big tower-looking building two or three hundred feet high. There is a large clock on the tower which tells the time. There is no image of Buddha inside this temple, where on every seventh day they worship what they call God who, in their faith, is the Creator of the World. There are many benches in the church on which people sit during the service. All the members of the church bring their Books to the service. The priest, on an elevated seat, tells his congregation to open the Book at such and such a place, and when this is done, the priest reads from the Book and he preaches the message of the text he has just read. The service over, they all leave the church. This kind of service is held also on board the ships.

Every year on the Fourth of July, they have a big celebration·throughout the land in commemoration of a great victory of their country over England in a war which took place seventy-five years ago. On that day they display the weapons which they used in the war. They put on the uniforms, and armed with swords and guns, they put up sham fights and then parade the streets and make a great rejoicing on that day.

Then Manjiro related his observations about the arms and ships of America, pointing out their superiority over Japanese arms and ships:

As the gun is regarded as the best weapon in America, they are well trained how to use it. When they go hunting they take small guns, but in war they use large guns since they are said to be more suitable for war. Ports and fortresses are protected by dozens of these large guns so that it would be extremely difficult to attack them successfully. Before Europeans came to America, the natives used bows and arrows, but these old-fashioned weapons proved quite powerless before firearms

which were brought by Europeans. Now the bow and arrow
has fallen into disuse in America. To the best of my knowledge, they have never used bamboo shields, as we do, although
they use sometimes the shields of copper plates for the protection of the hull of a fighting ship. They are not well trained
in swordsmanship or spearsmanship, however, so that in my
opinion, in close fighting, a samurai could easily take on three
Americans.

American men, even officials, do not carry swords as the
samurai do. But when they go on a journey, even common
men usually carry with them two or three pistols; their pistol
is somewhat equivalent to the sword of a samurai. As I said
before, their chief weapon is firearms and they are skillful in
handling them. Moreover, as they have made a thorough study
of the various weapons used by foreign armies, they believe
that there are hardly any foreign weapons that can frighten
them out of their wits.

Both a whaling ship and a fighting ship are built essentially
in the same way and the only difference is that the latter
carries guns. In other words, a whaling ship is strongly built
and can easily be converted into a fighting ship. Usually a
fighting ship is manned by about a hundred men, but in time
of war, this number can be increased to one thousand five
hundred men. A fighting ship of a certain type which is lightly
built can attain a high speed carrying several guns. A long-
boat can also be used as a fighting ship, because it can be fitted
with a three-inch gun to fight the enemy in a shallow sea right
up to the beach.

More and more both fighting ships and merchant ships
driven by the steam engine have been built of late in America.
These steamships can be navigated in all directions irrespective
of the current and wind and they can cover the distance of
two hundred *ri* a day. The clever device with which these
ships are built is something more than I can describe. While
in America I had no chance to learn the trade of shipbuilding,

so that I would not say that I can build one with confidence. Since I have looked at them carefully, however, I shall be able to direct our shipwrights to build one, if I could get hold of some foreign books on the subject.

I have sailed in my time on American whaling ships through the North and South Pacific Ocean, not to speak of Japanese waters, the South Seas, the Indian Ocean and the Atlantic Ocean; I have learnt the art of observing the heavenly bodies and the method of navigation. If I only had a large ship, I could sail it to any part of the world.

Then the official asked Manjiro about President Fillmore and Commodore Perry, but he found the names too difficult to pronounce. He read those names written in the Japanese syllabary which was pronounced something like President Hiruore and Commodore Peruri. So Manjiro said:

The way you pronounce the names of the President and his messenger, I gather that they are not Americans. Perhaps they are Dutchmen after all. I never heard such names while I was in America. The letter which is said to have been addressed to the Shogun by the President in question is highly suspicious. If I see the letter, however, I can instantly tell whether or not it is a genuine one. Be that as it may, it has been a long cherished desire on the part of America to establish friendly relations between Japan and that country, particularly in view of the fact that whenever an American vessel is shipwrecked in Japanese waters, the survivors are treated very harshly, as if they were so many beasts, by the Japanese authorities. The Americans think that the people of other countries should not be discriminated against, because they believe that the people of the world must live like brothers. Even when a ship belonging to a country with which America has no intercourse is wrecked, the survivors of the ship are always rescued and kindly treated by Americans. I can tell this from my own experience. They think that the establishment of friendly relations between Japan and America will put an end to the harsh treatment by the Japanese officials of the shipwrecked American sailors. I cannot understand, however, why they should ask in the said letter to open trade between the two countries, because America produces enough goods necessary for its people's living and also they know quite well that Japan can do without foreign trade.

While I was in America I did not hear any good or bad remarks in particular about our country but I did hear Americans say that the Japanese people were easily alarmed, even when they see a ship in distress approaching their shores for help, and how they shoot it on sight, when there was no real cause for alarm at all. I also heard them speak very highly of Japanese swords, which they believe that no other swords could possibly rival. I heard too that Yedo of Japan, together with Peking of China and London of England, are the three largest and finest cities of the world.

AN ERA
DAWNS

COMMODORE PERRY and his fleet which consisted of the *Susquehanna*, his flagship, the *Mississippi*, and the sloops-of-war *Saratoga* and *Plymouth*, suddenly appeared off the town of Uraga on July 8, 1853, to negotiate with the Japanese Government to "open the country to the rest of the world." On July 14, accompanied by his officers and escorted by a body of armed marines and sailors — in all about three hundred men — and while the band was playing he went ashore and presented to commissioners especially appointed by the Shogun his own credentials and a letter from President Fillmore to the Emperor. Fully aware of the importance of the occasion, the Yedo Government had massed two hundred flags and bunting bedecked boats in the bay and eight thousand full-dressed samurai near the landing place. But a few days later, at the polite but insistent request of the Japanese officials, the American fleet sailed for Hongkong with the understanding that it would return the following spring to receive the Emperor's reply.

At the news that the "black ships" had appeared in the Bay of Yedo, the island empire of centuries-old tranquil isolation was thrown into confusion and turmoil. A state of emergency had been declared in Yedo while the samurai, in battle array, guarded its seaboard and strategic points and the alerted firemen ran about the streets; the citizens were panic-stricken and women and children trembled and tried to run away from Yedo. The "loyalists" throughout the country stirred and demanded their "divine country" be kept inviolate from "barbarous foreigners" and opposed any attempt to conclude a treaty with them. The Tokugawa Government had to face a storm.

It sent a messenger posthaste to Tosa to ask Manjiro to come up to Yedo as quickly as possible to serve and save the country now confronted by a great crisis brought about by the visit of Commodore Perry's fleet. Although Manjiro was then teaching at one of the clan's schools in Tosa, he accepted the invitation from the Tokugawa Government thinking that he might be able to make himself more useful in Yedo with his knowledge of foreign countries. He left Kochi for Yedo on August 1, 1853.

On November 6, Lord Abe, who was a progressive cabinet member, appointed him a managing official worth twenty bushels of rice, with two retainers in his service. He was given the right to wear two swords like a regular samurai and the privilege of adopting the surname of Nakahama, from the name of his native place, Nakanohama, as his only name had been Manjiro like any other humble fisherman of the day. A fisherman's boy, who otherwise would have been destined to be a fisherman for the rest of his life under the centuries-old strict caste system, awoke one morning a great vassal to the Shogun!

When Manjiro came to Yedo at the request of the Shogun, he was kept in protective custody and no one was allowed to see him without official permission; the Shogun feared that any information originating from Manjiro could be used against the security of the country, which was threatened by the sudden appearance of Perry's fleet in Uraga Bay. Chief Secretary Egawa of the Department of Navigation, Survey and Shipbuilding filed the following petition with the Shogun in September, 1853:

At the time when Manjiro, who had lived in America, was summoned to Magistrate Kawaji's mansion for questioning, I had the occasion to be there, and put certain questions to him in regard to the matters I am anxious to know. If it please you, let him, therefore, come to my house two or three times to answer my questions in the presence of three or four learned men in my service.

But even the petition from such an important vassal was pigeonholed, so chary was the Shogun of Manjiro's being used for some inscrutable purpose. Chief Secretary Egawa, however, thought that Manjiro's service was of great value in his office and he repeatedly petitioned the Shogun to appoint Manjiro as his assistant, which at last was granted on November 22. As Egawa took great interest in Manjiro, he allowed him to live in the premises of his mansion in Honjo, Yedo, although the Shogun at first did not approve of this. Then he obtained official permission for the return to Manjiro of all the foreign articles which the government had confiscated from their rightful owner. Some of these things, particularly the scientific books, were very useful to him when he assisted Chief Secretary Egawa, the most enterprising engineering official of his day, and also when he taught many classes of aspiring students.

In the meantime, Commodore Perry reappeared in the Bay of Yedo with his fleet on February 11, 1854, and, despite the protests of the Japanese, selected an anchorage about twelve miles farther up the bay, nearly opposite Yokohama and within about ten miles of Yedo.

Again a state of emergency was declared, but this time the Yedo Government knew that it must face the inevitable and sign a treaty to open the country. On this occasion the Japanese officials even tried to be friendly with the Perry mission with good grace; they entertained the Commodore and his staff at a formal Japanese banquet in which *sake*, raw fish and many other strange things were served and they even allowed themselves to be invited to the flagship *Susquehanna* to taste the meat of "four-footed beasts." But when the Japanese officials saw sailors sing and dance in a minstrel show, they laughed and laughed, forgetting their usual dignity.

Commodore Perry presented to the Shogun a model train, a telegraphic apparatus, books, and in return the Shogun presented the fleet, among other things, with two hundred straw bags of rice and three hundred chickens. The officials took the occasion to impress the foreigners with the brawn of the Japanese people. They had brought together ninety-three professional wrestlers at Uraga and held exhibition matches in the traditional custom. Then all of the ninety-three wrestlers, each carrying a 130-pound straw bag of rice on each shoulder, proceeded to the landing place in procession. Many Japanese officials and people of Uraga were thrilled when they heard for the first time the band play marches and they asked the band to play more. They were also impressed, though unable to understand the device, by a telegraphic apparatus which the Americans demonstrated by stretching a mile-long wire on the beach.

The Tokugawa Government had invited Manjiro to Yedo with the intention of using him as an official interpreter and adviser for the negotiations with Commodore Perry. But on learning that Manjiro not only spoke English very fluently but advocated progressive ideas in favor of the opening of the country, isolationist elements in the government took exception to assigning such an important job to him. They feared that he might reveal some of the secrets of the country to the Americans and conclude the negotiations on their terms. They particularly feared that these barbarians might kidnap Manjiro and take him aboard one of the ships in an attempt to use him as a cat's-paw against the interests of the country, should Manjiro's usefulness be revealed to them.

Lord Nariaki of Mito, spiritual leader of the nationalist movement of his day, sent a letter to Egawa advising him to prevent Manjiro from coming into contact with the foreigners, which read something like this:

While there is no justification for doubting the character of Manjiro — a commendable person who has returned to this country for which he has a great attachment — those barbarians took advantage of his boyhood, bestowed special favors upon him alone by teaching him the art of counting. This may be construed as some insidious wile on the part of those barbarians. Moreover, as he had been saved by them and had

been under their care from his boyhood until he was twenty
years of age, he owes a debt of gratitude to them and, therefore, it is inconceivable that he should act contrary to their
interests.

Under no circumstances should he be permitted to go on
any one of the ships or meet those barbarians when they land,
even if you have thoroughly established that he is above suspicion. Nor is it advisable to let Manjiro know anything about
what we discuss.

Be that as it may, you might use your discretion and try to
get information about the barbarians in the hope of preventing
them from taking advantage by using Manjiro as a tool therefor.

The Lord of Mito advised in the postscript that Manjiro
should be placed under secret surveillance lest "a baby
dragon escape riding on the winds and clouds when a storm
comes." He also advised that Manjiro should be placed
under no constraint whatsoever but instead should be given
good treatment because, should he perchance become re-
sentful, his services could not be counted upon.

As a result, he was not allowed to meet anyone of Perry's
party and was kept behind the scenes. No one, of course,
could rival Manjiro in English and his knowledge of foreign
countries, but the government had to employ interpreters
who were not half so good. In fact, the negotiations were
mostly conducted in Dutch as the interpreters understood
Dutch better than English. It is recorded, however, that
their knowledge of Dutch was quite limited and almost
totally lacking in diplomatic terminology. Besides it was
as archaic as that of Grotius.

Manjiro apparently took the whole turn of events phil-
osophically, believing that it was no use exciting isolationist
elements in the government in the presence of Commodore

Perry. He knew that the odds were definitely against him and decided that all he could do under the circumstances was to teach his countrymen the facts about the rest of the world and open their eyes to modern science, believing that that was the best thing he could do in the interest of his country. Thus, although he secretly resented the government's measure to bar him from the negotiations with Commodore Perry's mission, he said to himself, The time will come soon when everything will be all right.

In the meantime, on March 31, 1854, there was concluded the first treaty, known as the Kanagawa Treaty, which among other things officially opened the ports of Shimoda and Hakodate to American ships, thus ending the old closed-door policy of Japan.

In spite of the Kanagawa treaty, Japan's doors actually remained closed to foreign commerce, and it was reserved for another citizen of America to open them. This was Townsend Harris (1803–78), the first U.S. consul general in Japan. Arriving in August, 1856, he concluded in June of the following year a treaty securing to American nationals the privilege of permanent residence at Shimoda and Hakodate, the opening of Nagasaki, the right of consular jurisdiction and certain minor concessions. Still, however, permission for commercial intercourse was withheld, and Harris, convinced that his great goal could not be reached unless he made his way to Yedo and conferred directly with the Shogun's ministers, pressed persistently for leave to do so. The Yedo administration was already weakened by the growth of a strong public sentiment in favor of abolishing the dual system of government — that of the Mikado in Kyoto and that of the Shogun in Yedo. Openly to sanction commercial relations at such a time would have been little short of disastrous. The Perry treaty and the first Harris treaty could be construed as mere acts of benevolence toward strangers; but a commercial treaty would not have lent itself to any such construction, and naturally the Shogun's ministers hesitated to agree to an apparently suicidal step. Harris carried his point, however. He was received by the Shogun in Yedo in November, 1857, and on July 29, 1858, a treaty was signed in Yedo, agreeing that Yokohama should be opened July 4, 1859, and the commerce between the United States and Japan should thereafter be freely carried on there.

In 1854, the year when Commodore Perry revisited Japan, Manjiro married, through a go-between, a pretty seventeen-year-old daughter of Gennosuke Danno, who owned and taught in a fencing school in Honjo not far from Egawa's mansion where Manjiro was living. Her name was Tetsu and although she had an elder sister who was as pretty and demure as any samurai's daughter, the go-between thought that the younger one, who was more vivacious than her elder sister, was more suitable for the young man who had lived in America for many years.

Before Manjiro married the pretty daughter of the fencing instructor, he had often thought that he would marry a girl he loved, as was the Western custom. But he found that it was almost impossible, for no respectable maiden would let herself love a young man unless she were engaged to marry him. In those days honorable marriages were arranged by go-betweens at the request, or with the approval of the parents, often even against the girl's will. Manjiro could not bring himself to follow this custom blindly. So after his engagement to the girl was arranged, he met her alone several times. One day he took her for a

walk around the duck pond in Egawa's mansion. Looking
at the stars reflected in the duck pond, the girl asked Manjiro, "Why do they say that good girls should not fall in
love?"

"Because it is our custom, but a custom will change."

"Do American girls fall in love before they marry?"

"Yes, they usually do."

"I think Japanese girls begin to love after they marry;
of course, I mean, their husbands." Then she asked, "Is it
all right for a girl to fall in love before she is married?"

"I think it's natural in a country like America."

Then they walked together along the shore of the starlit
pond in the Japanese garden. Her prettiness in the summer
kimono was still visible in the darkness. At a bend of the
lane, he held her firmly and kissed her.

"We are very happy, aren't we?"

"Oh, I am the happiest girl in all Yedo," said Tetsu, smiling coyly.

About this time, Lord Abe had the *Adventure,* in which
Manjiro had reached Ryukyu, brought around from Nagasaki to Yedo for inspection. Subsequently several longboats
were built after this model which became the prototype of
modern Japanese longboats. Lord Abe was a statesman of
great caliber and was promoted to be a member of the
Cabinet when he was only twenty-five years of age. Among
many important vassals to the Shogun, no one could rival
him in ability, popularity and personality, so that Lord Ii
and Lord Izumi of the rival faction, who became jealous
of the great reputation of this young official, hated him and
plotted to oust him. So the latter always carried a resignation in his pocket, ready to tender it at any moment's notice.

Lord Abe knew that Japan could no longer remain iso-

lated from the rest of the world and appointed Tarozaemon
Egawa to a position of supervising the sea defenses and other
engineering works and invited Manjiro to come to Yedo
from Tosa to advise the government. In full realization of
the necessity of making a survey of Japanese waters and of
learning the art of navigation, as soon as he appointed Manjiro as assistant to Egawa, he instructed Manjiro to submit
a report on his own plan of developing the sea power of this
nation. He also instructed Manjiro to translate E. C.
Branter's book on navigation which he had brought from
America and after two years' painstaking work he completed the translation, and greatly contributed to the art of
navigation in Japan. In 1855, Egawa suddenly died. In the
meantime, Lord Abe, whose health declined considerably,
at last tendered his resignation and was succeeded by
Masamitsu Hotta. Two years later in 1857, Lord Abe also
died in the prime of his life at the age of thirty-nine. Thus
Manjiro lost in less than two years two great patrons who
understood and encouraged him in all his undertakings
when others distrusted him. Indeed, had it not been for
these patrons, he might have ended his life in obscurity in
Kochi.

In April, 1857, Manjiro became an instructor at the Naval
Training School which was established at Yedo that year
and taught navigation and ship engineering to many trainees
who were destined to be important figures in the Japanese
Navy. Then in October of the following year, he proceeded,
by order, to Hakodate in Hokkaido to serve in the governor's
office as a whaling instructor. While there, he probed the
possibility of starting a whaling industry in that area. He
returned to Yedo in the spring of 1859. He was quite busy
that year; he compiled A *Short Cut To English Conversa-*

tion, which became the standard book on practical English in those days. It was superior to all the other books on the subject already in circulation, because through the proper use of the Japanese alphabet, it enabled the student to pronounce English much more accurately than any other book of its kind at that time.

Earlier, he had proposed that the government undertake a whaling business believing that not only could it be a profitable enterprise but it would afford a good chance to train young men in navigation and sounding. This proposal was eventually approved by the government and he was appointed supervisor of the proposed whaling enterprise in 1859. He at once set about the task of fitting out a schooner called the *Kimigata I* which had been presented to the Tokugawa Government by the Russian Government. He painted it black, built a crow's-nest, and installed proper equipment for processing whales. He supervised the construction of the whaleboats at Ishikawajima and trained about twenty fishermen from Ajiro who were to man the whaling ship. All this while he continued teaching English to his students.

The entry in his diary under the date of July 29, 1859, reads:

Mr. Egawa and I went by boat to Ishikawajima, the site of the ship-building. We rested in one of the whaleboats, then went to inspect the Russian ship off Shinagawa. Returned home very late.

Seeing officials, visiting the shipyard, training the crew, teaching English, Manjiro spent busy days, but he was happy because the preparations for another whaling voyage were making good progress. The September 18 entry in the diary says:

Fair weather and moderate winds. All well with the world. The family are safe and sound. The two shipwrights of Tosa came to see me. Mr. Otori came to learn English.

As soon as the preparations were completed in March, he set sail from Shinagawa, thrilled with the foretaste of hunting whales in the Pacific, a thing he had dreamed about for many years. But before a single whale was caught, the expedition completely failed. The schooner was overtaken by a storm near the Ogasawara Islands and only with great difficulty did he manage to return to the port of Shimoda after cutting down one of the masts. When the storm blew over, he navigated the crippled schooner into the Bay of Shinagawa for repair to make another attempt to go whaling.

A
GOODWILL
MISSION

About this time, the Tokugawa Government decided to send a goodwill mission to America for the ratification of the treaty which had been concluded between Townsend Harris and the government. Manjiro was appointed official interpreter and instructor in navigation to be sent with the party sailing on the *Kanrin-maru*.

The mission, consisting of seventy-seven men headed by Lord Chikami and Lord Muragaki, left Shinagawa on board the U.S. warship *Powhatan* in February, 1860. Simultaneously, a Japanese warship, the *Kanrin-maru*, sailed from Uraga for America, carrying Lord Kimuru, Captain Rintaro Katsu, Yukichi Fukuzawa, Manjiro and about ninety other men. This man-of-war, which the Tokugawa Government had purchased from Holland, was equipped with an auxiliary engine of one hundred horsepower and was a convenient ship in which both new and old combined — a steamer in home waters and a sailing vessel in the high seas.

The *Powhatan* touched at Honolulu, while the *Kanrin-maru* sailed straightway for San Francisco, reaching there on March 17, 1860. It was a long stormy passage and only Manjiro's skill to navigate the ship prevented it from being shipwrecked. A newspaper of that city carried the following article:

A Japanese warship, the *Kanrin-maru,* made port at San Francisco at 3 o'clock yesterday afternoon after a successful voyage of thirty-seven days since she left Uraga, Japan, under the direction of Captain Katsu. Lord Kimura, admiral of the Japanese Navy, is among the passengers on board the ship. It is learned that the ship is acting as a sort of harbinger to the *Powhatan,* that is now en route to this country, charged with the important mission of transporting the Japanese Ambassadors.

The admiral is always followed by four retainers who are ready to wait upon him most reverently. But he seems to know better than to treat them like slaves. Some of the crew, who wore straw sandals, were eying us curiously from the deck. These men seemed to be far better-mannered than the Chinese in California. As we boarded the ship, we were much struck by its cleanness and apple-pie orderliness. We had the pleasure of meeting Lord Kimura in his cabin. He seemed to be entrusted with the important mission. When we entered his room, he squatted while one of the servants was trying to do up a most elegant coiffure for the lord. Soon he appeared on the deck in his formal dress: a pair of pure white socks, a dark brown coat, and a blue skirt — all of excellent quality. He wore two swords at his side. All the officials wore beautiful swords, sharp and shining . . .

The American newspapers featured the arrival of the vessel showing affection as well as curiosity for the Japanese. The strange customs of the Japanese were a constant source of interest.

Lord Kimura and his party landed at San Francisco for the first time and were escorted to the International Hotel. In the lobby they formally met the Mayor of San Francisco and other dignitaries of the city. It was a curious sight to see all the Japanese officials squatted on the floor except Lord Kimura, who sat on the sofa when Governor John G. Downey of California appeared to greet the strangers. It passed their comprehension to see the Governor appear alone without being followed by a solemn procession of his retainers. They thought him to be an impersonator. It was only when Captain Brook, an aide to the Governor, repeatedly endeavored to explain that the man was the real Governor that at last they exchanged greetings with him through the interpretation of Manjiro who spoke English very fluently. The Governor expressed his congratulations on the occasion of the two nations, separated by the Pacific, entering upon a new friendly relationship to open trade between them.

Lord Kimura and Captain Katsu, shaking hands with everyone present, bowed politely in Japanese style, while Manjiro acted as interpreter. When the name and the office of the man to be introduced was announced by Manjiro, Lord Kimura received him in a gentlemanly and refined manner. The occasion was an important affair even for America, for it was an epoch-making event in the history of America-Japan relations, so the U.S. Government and the public tried to give the Japanese a warm welcome. On that day each Japanese wore a fine dress and two swords, but the costume of Lord Kimura was particularly beautiful. The Japanese costume is entirely different from that of the Chinese. A banquet was held in the great hall of the hotel in honor of the Japanese. They ate a small portion of each dish, but they seemed to be quite satisfied. Captain Katsu, when served with ice cream, said, "I have never tasted such a wonderful thing in my life."

Captain Katsu speaks English fairly well but not so well as Manjiro, official interpreter, who speaks English fluently as he was educated in Fairhaven, Mass., when he was a boy. Captain Katsu is never seen with a hat on. The temple of his head is shaven, and his hair, which is sticking up like black needles, is tied at the end so that it is pointing forward. All the officials have their hair in like manner. Half a dozen smart-looking officials have wide-brimmed white hats resembling those worn by the Chinese in California on a rainy day. The rest of them put on straw bonnets with string which go under their chins lest they should be blown off.

While in San Francisco, the Japanese officials received every attention from the citizens as well as the officials. One of the peculiarities first manifested by the foreign dignitaries was a disinclination to regard women as equals, in consequence of which the feminine sex was forbidden to set foot on their vessel. This is said to have been owing less to adherence to their own prejudices than to a misapprehension of the social position of women in America.

The party of delegates, after San Francisco's warm reception, boarded the *Powhatan* again for Panama. Crossing the Isthmus by train, they boarded the *Roanoke*, an American man-of-war, and eventually reached Washington. They were accorded a rousing welcome there as the official guests of the U.S. Government. Sixty rooms of the Willard Hotel, one of the best hotels in Washington, were placed at their disposal, and great banquets were held in their honor. In short, it was as warm a welcome as ever the U.S. Government and the U.S. Army and Navy had given to any foreign delegation.

Lord Chikami and Lord Muragaki were received in audience by President Buchanan and they exchanged the notes of ratification of the Japanese-American Treaty. On May 13, they received a gala send-off from the American public and embarked on the Niagara (4580 tons), one of the largest ships of America at that time, and via the Cape of Good Hope, Java, and Hong Kong, the party returned safely to Shinagawa.

In the meantime the *Kanrin-maru*, which had been badly damaged by a storm when crossing the Pacific, had to be docked for repair at the Mare Island Navy Yard near San Francisco. While in San Francisco, Manjiro bought many "articles of civilization," such as a sewing machine and a daguerreotype apparatus with which he became the first photographer in Yedo. He particularly wanted to take a picture of his mother. But photography (daguerreotype) was still in a crude and primitive stage and it produced a picture of a man whose kimono appeared "left-side-front." So before anyone had a picture taken of himself, he had to wear his kimono actually "left-side-front" and his swords on the right side of his waist in order to appear properly dressed. Manjiro and Yukichi Fukuzawa, who was later to found Keio University, each bought a Webster's dictionary, the first two English dictionaries ever openly imported into Japan.

Ten years before, during the hectic days of the Gold Rush, Manjiro had waited in San Francisco for a ship to take him to Honolulu and thence home. In 1850, San Francisco was a city of tents, shanties with goods, boxes and barrels strewn all over the place and sunk in the liquid mud of the streets. At that time, the population suddenly grew from two thousand to twenty thousand in less than a year as steamers one after another arrived with emigrants from the East over the Isthmus. Manjiro had seen more than five hundred vessels lying in the bay, most of them deserted by their crews. Many rotted, others were beached, and were converted into stores and lodging houses. He knew a street corner where he had seen a signboard saying, "No man, not even a fool, can walk on this street." It was a booming but filthy town, full of outlaws who took the law into their hands while the city government was too corrupt and inefficient to repress them. Now he was struck with the orderliness of the town where there had been no order. It had grown into a fine prosperous city with stone or brick buildings and wide streets, where decent-looking and law-abiding men and women thronged. He remembered that gold dust, then private coins, and money of various countries had been in circulation but now the banks refused to accept foreign coins. While he was in San Francisco in 1860, he saw mail communication established with the East by a pony express, the charge being five dollars for a half-ounce letter.

The *Kanrin-maru,* on her homeward voyage, put in at Honolulu where the party was received in audience by King Kamehameha. Manjiro visited Toraemon, the cooper, and other old acquaintances in Honolulu for the first time in eleven years. They were greatly surprised to see him wearing a large and a small sword like a brave samurai and said gladly, "John Mung has risen in the world."

He also went to see the Reverend Samuel Damon, whom he always remembered gratefully, because if it had not been for this kindly preacher who raised the money for their boat, Manjiro and the others might have been unable to return to Japan safely. The pastor could hardly recognize him at first and was much pleased to learn that Manjiro had become a fine-looking official of the Japanese Government.

While Manjiro was in Honolulu, he wrote a letter to Captain Whitfield and asked the pastor to send it to him by a special mail ship bound for Fairhaven, Massachusetts, along with a kimono as a souvenir:

Sandwich Island, May 2, 1860.

Captain William H. Whitfield,

My Honored Friend — I am very happy to say that I had an opportunity to say to you a few lines. I am still living and hope you were the same blessing. I wish to meet you in this world once more. How happy we would be. Give my best respect to Mrs. and Miss Amelia Whitfield, I long to see them. Capt. you must not send your boys to the whaling business; you must send them to Japan, I will take care of him or them if you will. Let me know before send and I will make the arrangement for it.

Now I will let you know that I have been to the Gold Mine; here stayed 4 months, average eight dollars per day, beside expenses, from here I made up my mind to get back and to see Dear Mother and also shipped in one of the American merchantmen. In this vessel I arrived at Sandwich Island. I found our friend Mr. Damon and through his kindness bought whale boat and put her into a merchantman. This vessel was going to Shanghai in China.

It was January very cold that part of country; Time I went on shore south off Great Loo Choo it was gail with snow. The Capt. of vessel he wish me to stay with him and to go to China, but I refused it, because I wanted to see Mother.

The boat is ready for me to get in, myself, Dennozo & Goyeman jump into the boat, parted with ship at 4 P.M. After ten hours hard pull we arrived lee of Island and anchored until morning. I went on shore amongst the Loo Choose, but I cannot understand their language, I have forgot all Japanese words. I stay here six months, under care of the King of Loo Choo, waiting for Japanese junk to come.

In the month of July get on board junk and went into the
harbour Nagashirki Island, off Kie-u-see-u, waiting to get permission for 30 months before we get to our residence. After
all the things is properly regulated we were sent to our residence.
It was great joy to Mother and all the relation. I have stay
with my Mother only 3 days and night the Emperor called
me to Jedo. I became one emperian officer. At this time I am
attached this vessel.

This war steamer was sent by Emperor of Japan to the com-
pliment of the President of America. We went to San Francisco, California, and now homeward bound, at Sandwich to
touch Island to secure some coal and provition. I wish to send
the letter from San Francisco but so many Japanese eyes I
can't. I wrote this between passage from San Francisco to
Island. Excuse me many mistakes. I can write better after
our arrived Japan Jedo.

I wish for you to come to Japan, I will now lead my Dear
Friend to my house, now the port opened to all the nations.
I found our friend Samuel C. Damon. We are so happy each
other I cannot write it all. When get home I will write better
account. I will send to you suit of my clothe. It is not new,
but only for remember me.

I remain your friend,

JOHN MUNGERO (May 25, 1860)

The Reverend Samuel Damon also wrote a letter to Captain Whitfield telling all about his impression of John
Mung "dressed like a Japanese official with two swords,"
who had come to see him when the homebound *Kanrin-
maru* touched at Honolulu. He sent this letter together
with John Mung's to Captain Whitfield.

Captain W. H. Whitfield,
Dear Sir, — Accompanying this letter I forward you a communication from your protégé, John Mung, the Japanese. You

will be doubtless as much surprised to hear from him as I was to see him. I have written out an account of his visit to Honolulu for the next No. of "The Friend." This I shall send to you, and it will furnish you the information which I am confident will be most interesting to you. He speaks of you with the most grateful feelings and also of your family. He wished to learn all about your children. I have taken the liberty to read the letter, which he left with me for you, and also to retain a copy of the same. It is a very great source of satisfaction to me to have seen him again. For years I have striven to learn something about him, but I could not obtain the least information. Judge then of my great surprise to have him come to my study, dressed like a Japanese official, with "his two swords."

He was very free and communicative, often called, and brought the captain of the steamer, who was a man of much intelligence. John has really become a man of importance in Japan. I could not state in print all he told me about his position, but let me say that it is my decided opinion that John Mung acted a most important part in opening Japan. The information which he furnished the Japanese Government was of immense importance. His translation of Bowditch's *Navigator* is most remarkable. [Some think that the book must have been E. C. Branter's book on navigation.]

He left with me to be forwarded to you a suit of his Japanese costume! Unless I can send it by some gentlemen going overland, I will forward the same by some New Bedford whaleship.

I have become so much interested in John that I want you to write me and tell me when and where you first found him, for I am quite astonished at the ability which he displays.

I think when you write him you had better send your letter to my care, for we have frequent opportunities of sending letters to Japan. A vessel, the *Leo*, arrived from Japan today. Do you feel like paying a visit? He is placed in a position where he is constantly watched, in other words, there are "many eyes in Japan," so he says. The reason why he had not written us has been that he could not get his letters out of the country. He told me that at the end of two years, or when Yedo was open to foreigners that he hoped I would visit Japan. He offered me the hospitality of his house.

Your honorable friends, the Diamonds, the Smithes, the Damons, the Harris (the lawyers) are all well.

Now, I shall expect a letter from you and if you send one for John Mung, alias Captain Mungero, etc., I will send it to him by the very earliest opportunity.

Yours,

Sam C. Damon

P.S. Remember to your fellow townsman,
Cap. S. Cox and family.

AFTER
YEARS

MANJIRO returned to Japan on board the *Kanrin-maru* on June 24, 1860, but something unexpected was in store for him. The captain of a certain American ship staying at Yokohama invited him to the ship to celebrate his safe return from America. Without fully realizing the consequences that followed the fraternizing with foreigners, who were still looked upon with suspicion and fear in Japan, John accepted the invitation and went. Punishment followed. He was summarily dismissed from the post of instructor to the Navy, which he had held for three years.

Although he was for the time in the bad graces of the Tokugawa Government, a few months later, in recognition of the great service he had rendered during the trip to America, the government awarded him fifty pieces of silver, two suits of silk clothes, several *koku* of rice, and other things.

In October of the following year, however, Manjiro returned to government service as chief interpreter and technical adviser for an official party sailing on the *Kanrin-maru* for the Ogasawara Islands to carry out a survey and proclaim Japanese sovereignty over those islands. About fifty stranded foreigners, who were living on these islands, were glad at the sight of the ship which brought along food and medical supplies, and they willingly helped the party do its task. The mission having been successfully accomplished, the party returned to Shinagawa in March of the following year.

It happened that the measles raged in Yedo in 1862, and his wife Tetsu caught the disease while she was in childbed. Despite all efforts to cure her, she passed away at the age of twenty-five, to the great sorrow of her husband and three children. Manjiro, brokenhearted, wanted to forget his sorrow by going on a whaling voyage.

He had always had an irresistible longing to sail a schooner in chase of whales instead of remaining as an official in the Tokugawa Government, the days of which were numbered. He proposed a whaling expedition to a wealthy merchant from Echigo, Renzo Hirano by name, and succeeded in getting his financial support for his long-cherished desire to be a whaler. In 1862, he was appointed captain of the *Ichiban-maru*. Loaded with shipbuilding materials and necessary equipment, the ship left Shinagawa in December, the same year, and reached the port of Futami in Ogasawara Island in January of the following year. The expedition started building two whale boats with the materials which had been brought along from Shinagawa, and in two months they were successfully launched. On March 17, carrying these boats, the *Ichiban-maru* finally set about whaling in the neighboring waters and by the middle of April they had caught two sperm whales.

It happened, however, that there was a ferocious rogue by the name of William Smith, British by nationality, among the foreign sailors whom Manjiro had hired at Ogasawara. He committed all sorts of violence and tried to steal everything valuable in sight. One day, Smith and another rogue attempted to steal goods from the ship at the point of a pistol, but Captain Manjiro Nakahama proved a perfect master of the situation and, with the help of his men, he thwarted the attempt and finally put them under arrest. He could have taken the law into his own hands but fearing any rash action on his part might give rise to some international complication, he locked up the men in a cabin of the ship and, much as he regretted doing so, he left Ogasawara waters on May 1 for Uraga to deliver them to the British legation there.

Then Manjiro unloaded the barrels of whale oil and made preparations for another expedition. However, this time the government would not permit the ship to leave the port, on the ground that the international situation was getting too critical to warrant such an expedition.

Indeed, the international situation had been bad enough for some time. Earlier, in 1859, Governor Muraviev of Eastern Siberia, accompanied by his fleet of ten warships, came close to Shinagawa to negotiate on his own terms with the Tokugawa Government about the Saghalien border and fishery rights. It happened that a Russian officer and two sailors from the fleet were attacked by several Japanese and fatally wounded in Yokohama. This incident deadlocked the negotiations and Muraviev and all his ships but one suddenly left the Bay of Yedo.

He dispatched a man-of-war, the *Posadnik,* and another

one to Tsushima in the Korean Straits in 1861. Taking
advantage of the defenseless island, the Russians cut down
trees, surveyed the coast, built their houses and even mur-
dered a samurai. Thoroughly helpless, the Tokugawa Government asked the British Minister to Japan to mediate,
and it was only through his intervention that the Russian
warships left.

The situation took a turn for the worse in 1863. The
raging movement for expelling foreigners culminated in
firing on foreign ships at Shimonoseki and murdering and
injuring British subjects near Yokohama. In retaliation
British men-of-war bombarded the fortifications of the
Choshu and Satsuma Daimyos and completely routed their
samurai. These British operations finally convinced the
Japanese of their impotence in the face of Western arma-
ments and shattered their faith in the Tokugawa Government. Thus the year 1863 saw the nation suddenly roused
to the disintegrating effects of the feudal system. The
traditional antipathy to foreigners gave way to the desire
to study their civilization and adopt its best features. What
Manjiro had forewarned actually came to pass, and he was
inwardly glad that the morning of civilization was beginning
to dawn in Japan at last.

While the Tokugawas' power and fame were thus fast
ebbing and the cry "Down with the Tokugawa Government" was growing louder and louder, the Choshu Rebel-
lion broke out in 1865, proving once and for all the utter
incompetence of that government. Thus the situation
quickly got out of control and the general trend of events
pointed to the inevitable collapse of its power.

Under these circumstances Manjiro abandoned, at least
temporarily, the whaling voyage and stayed on Egawa's

premises in Honjo. He busied himself translating the table of logarithms and teaching English, mathematics and navigation to a class of scholars, officials and ambitious young men who had pronounced English in an absurd way before they received his instruction. Among his students were, to name a few, Fukuzawa, Hosokawa, Enomoto, Mitsukuri, and Otori, the men who later played important roles in the making of modern Japan as statesmen, generals, admirals, educators, diplomats and scientists. In fact, most of the great men who successfully served the country in the early years of the Meiji Era were directly or indirectly under Manjiro's influence at one time or another. He taught many young men wherever he went, in Tosa, in Kagoshima, in Hakodate and in Yedo, and his teaching gave rise to a chain reaction in political, educational, and scientific circles and quickened the tempo of modernizing Japan.

About this time, the Satsuma clan felt the need for training its clansmen in more modern methods of navigation and military science. It had taken a severe beating when a British fleet bombarded its fortifications in 1863. Also, in the same year, it had lost most of its well-trained navigators when the *Nagasaki-maru* was sunk by the coastal artillery of Choshu, the rival feudatory of Satsuma. The Satsuma Daimyo at once purchased several ships from abroad to rebuild its navy and sought Manjiro's assistance to train the clansmen to man those ships. The Yedo Government sent Manjiro to Satsuma in 1864.

Manjiro began teaching at the Kaisei-jo School in Kagoshima in the summer of that year and then he took leave of absence and went to Tosa to see his mother in January, 1866. There he stayed for about three months, during which time he had a neat and cozy house built for his mother. At the end of the three months, after a big send-off by the villagers, he went to Kochi, capital of Tosa, at the invitation of the Lord of Tosa. There he was asked to advise the Daimyo concerning establishment of a school called Kaisei-kan in Kochi and teach there. In March of that year, the school was opened and in July, when it was fairly well established, he decided to return to Kagoshima. He went to Nagasaki first, accompanied by Shojiro Goto, for they had been commissioned to buy a foreign ship at Nagasaki for the Daimyo of Tosa. But as there was no good ship to buy at that port, they went to Shanghai in August, where they bought a suitable ship and returned to Nagasaki.

At that time, Nagasaki was the most important trading center of Japan and the port was bustling with foreign ships and merchants. While there, Manjiro spent busy days negotiating with foreign traders to buy ships and weapons, sometimes for the Tokugawa Government, and other times for the Tosa Daimyo or the Kagoshima Daimyo. It happened that a fleet of three warships of Satsuma, led by the chief minister, put in at Nagasaki in September and so Manjiro at once went to see them and asked his permission to return to Yedo before he went to Kagoshima, for he had been away from home for about two and a half years. Before he actually returned to Yedo in December, 1866, however, he went to Shanghai again in October to oversee the construction of a ship in a shipyard there. In February, 1867, he returned to Kagoshima and resumed teaching its clansmen in navigation and whaling at the Kaisei-jo until November of that year when he finally returned to Yedo.

Almost immediately after the Meiji Restoration, which took place in 1868, the capital had been moved from Kyoto to Yedo, which was rechristened Tokyo. The Emperor

Meiji, who had come to the throne in 1867 when he was only sixteen years old, moved to Tokyo. All the fiefs and lands under the control of the Tokugawa came under the direct authority of the new government. Although anti-foreignism had served to oust the Shogun, as soon as the new government came into existence not only were friendly overtures made to foreign powers but Japan attempted to entirely remodel herself on European lines. Gradually, promising youths were sent abroad to study, and foreign experts were engaged and the foundations of the Meiji Government were gradually secured. Manjiro's dream at last came true.

A

REUNION

WHEN THE Tokugawa regime collapsed in 1868, many vassals lost their jobs and had to leave Yedo to seek their fortune in other provinces. However, Manjiro, whose reputation had been fully established by then, was appointed by the new government the same year instructor of the Kaisei-jo School, predecessor of the present Tokyo University.

The following year he left Egawa's Mansion to live at one of the official residences of the Tosa clan in Fukagawa and there he lived for the next thirteen years. The area was an extensive secluded domain with a large duck pond, where Manjiro often enjoyed duck hunting.

In September, 1870, Manjiro was ordered by the government to proceed to Europe with Iwao Oyama, who became later a field-marshal, and the supreme commander of the

Japanese army at the time of the Russo-Japanese War,
Yajiro Shinagawa, who became later a member of the Privy
Council, and twenty-four other Japanese, to make a firsthand observation of the Franco-Prussian War. The party
left Yokohama on September 4 on board the *Great Republic*
and after spending about one month crossing the Pacific, it
reached San Francisco. Manjiro had visited the city ten
years before and he had noticed then that it had changed
from the town of shanties, outlaws and fortune hunters
which he remembered so well when he had been there ten
years before that. He could not but be deeply impressed by
the rapidity with which the city was still further expanding.
When the party of Japanese officials came upon Market
Street, with stately stone or brick buildings on both sides,
crowded with people and carriages, both Oyama and Shinagawa were breathless with amazement. But Manjiro, acting
as a guide, tried to look unruffled like the experienced man
that he was and sagely explained many a strange thing to
them. As it happened, the city was in the "silver era," and
Manjiro found an excitement in the air paralleling that of
the Gold Rush which he knew so well.

The party stayed in San Francisco for two days and then
took a train for Chicago, which was already a commercial
center of immense importance having a population of over
three hundred thousand. The city was full of wooden
houses which were doomed to be reduced to ashes about a
year later by the Great Fire of 1871. The party stopped over
at Niagara Falls for sightseeing and reached New York on
October 28.

There were only five days left before the *Minnesota* which
was to take the party across the Atlantic to Southampton,
England, was scheduled to sail from New York, and Man-

jiro was busy making preparations for the voyage as well as taking his fellow countrymen over the city.

"I have a long-cherished desire which I'd like to fulfill," said Manjiro to Oyama.

"What can it possibly be?"

"As you know, I was rescued by an American whaleship when I was shipwrecked off the coast of Tosa about thirty years ago. The kindhearted captain of that ship took me to Fairhaven, his native town, and looked after me and put me in school. I owe him a great debt of gratitude. He lives in Fairhaven, not very far from here. With your permission, I'd like to go there and see him. *That* is what I mean by my long-cherished desire."

Oyama knew that he and Shinagawa would surely be at a loss in this great strange city without Manjiro, but he simply said, "Go, by all means," and he added, "We'll try to manage without you, if it is only a day or two."

On the morning of October 30, Manjiro took the train for New Bedford from New York. As it happened, New England's autumn was at its best. The woods of maple trees were aflame under the blue sky, and the hills were covered with wine-dark bracken and blueberry. As the train sped through the glorious autumnal countryside, he was exhilarated and drank in every bit of the ever changing train-side view. Every minute seemed to heighten the excitement of the reunion with the Whitfield family and the rest of his former friends. He felt then as though he were going to see his father from whom he had been absent for a long time. Arriving at New Bedford, he walked along the familiar streets toward Fairhaven like a man who was walking along his home-town streets for the first time in twenty years. When he crossed the long bridge over the Acushnet River and breathed the same old sea breeze and saw the same old harbor and the same old Mr. Bartlett's School where he studied mathematics for the first time in his life, a flood of memory rushed back to him and his heart ached. It was already late afternoon when he knocked on the door of Captain Whitfield's house.

"If it is not John Mung!" exclaimed Captain Whitfield with great excitement and delight. He shook hands vigorously with Manjiro and led him inside.

"I have been looking forward to this day for twenty years," said Manjiro, falteringly, tears in his eyes.

"It does my old heart good to see you again, John Mung," Captain Whitfield said in a choking voice. "Congratulations! You seem to have certainly risen in the world."

At first Captain and Mrs. Whitfield felt a little strange and embarrassed when they saw Manjiro, well dressed and dignified, but before very long they found that the Manjiro in front of them had little changed from the polite, cheerful, alert lad they remembered so well.

Manjiro told the captain about his experiences in detail. In the meantime, Marcellus, who was nineteen years old, son of Captain Whitfield, and a pretty daughter were introduced to Manjiro. They were both pleased to see the man whom their parents had often talked about so warmly. When Manjiro told them quaint stories about Japan and the Japanese people, they all seemed deeply interested and asked him all sorts of questions about the country and people.

"I hope someday you will be able to come to our country and see for yourselves what I've told you about," said Manjiro.

In the meantime, word that John Mung had come spread

all over the town, and soon all the neighbors, even those who did not know him, as well as his former friends, including Jean Allen, Eben Akin, Bartlett, Bonney, and others came to see the unexpected visitor. Soon Captain Whitfield's home was beseiged by a large crowd of people. Mrs. Whitfield and her daughter worked hard in the kitchen to prepare refreshments which they served to all. It was a happy reunion!

"It's so good to see you again," Manjiro told them. "I have always been thankful to you for every kindness you showed me a long while back. I've remembered it all this time. Since I returned to my country, I've been telling my countrymen how advanced your country is and that Japan has much to learn from you. They thought that I did not know what I was talking about at first. Now they are beginning to see for themselves. I'm glad to tell you that my country has recently opened her long-closed doors to the outside world and is ready to adopt Western civilization." Then Manjiro told them more of the strange customs and manners of his country, which they all thought fascinating. When he told them that Japanese men have a strange hairdo somewhat resembling a pistol, they all laughed. Then Manjiro gave Captain Whitfield and his family and all his former friends many presents which he had brought along from Japan — lacquer boxes, silk cloth, kimonos, Japanese color prints. They all admired the beauty of those articles.

"I sometimes think how I wish I could go with Captain Whitfield to catch whales again!" said Manjiro a little later.

"My dear John, perhaps, you are thinking of those good old days but you must know that times have changed a great deal since then," said the captain with a little bitterness. "You see, the discovery of oil fields in the Western States, and the Civil War in which we lost many ships, have dealt us a hard blow from which it will take a long time to recover."

"That accounts for the fact that the harbor was so quiet," said Manjiro.

"Now that the sperm whales are getting scarce," the old captain continued, "both in the Atlantic and the Pacific, some of our ships are planning to go whaling in the Arctic Ocean in great force next year. They say that that ocean is well stocked with bowhead whales, but it would be risky business to catch whales in a sea full of icebergs. Let young whalers go where they will. I've done enough dangerous whaling in my time."

That night when the visitors had all gone home and the family had retired to bed, the old sea captain and his former cabin boy talked on and on far into the night. They reminisced over their bygone adventures and discussed other subjects in which they were mutually interested. The time they could spend together was too short.

The following day, Manjiro, with tears in his eyes, said goodbyes to Captain Whitfield, his family and friends who were on hand to see him off, and let the town for New York. On the train back to New York, he thought to himself, I am glad that I took this opportunity to revisit Fairhaven and see those nice people again.

The *Morning Mercury* of New Bedford reported Manjiro's revisit to Fairhaven under the date November 1, 1870, as follows:

Personal: We had the pleasure of a call, yesterday, from Nakahama Mungero, a Japanese and one of the commission of seven appointed by the government of Japan to visit Europe and observe the warlike movements there. Mr. Mungero, with his associates, arrived in New York in 42 days from Yedo . . .

Arriving at New York, he lost no time in coming here to visit his old friends Capt. Whitfield and wife, for whom he expresses the most affectionate regard and to whose kindness he refers his success in life.

Mr. Mungero is 45 years of age, of short stature, but erect and vigorous, and with a face full of intelligence. He is fully fitted for the part assigned to him in the commission, the result of whose observations abroad cannot fail to benefit Japan. It is interesting to note in these facts the important and intimate connection between the whaling enterprise and the opening of Japan to the commerce of the world. The education of the wrecked Japanese boy at a public school in Fairhaven, through the kindness of a whaling captain, contributed materially to the establishment of the relations existing between this country and Japan.

The party, headed by Iwao Oyama, reached London safely on November 17 when the Franco-Prussian War was at its climax and the city of Paris itself threatened. But while the party was staying in London, just before it proceeded to the Continent, Manjiro was taken ill with a tumor which had developed in one of his feet. It turned out to be a rather serious case so that he had to be confined to the hotel room while the rest of the party set out on the last lap of their journey. He meant to rejoin the party as soon as he got well. But his strength returned too slowly, and he had to return to Japan alone in the spring of 1871.

He recuperated in his residence in Fukagawa and in a few months he was fairly strong again. He again conducted a class in his residence where many students came to study English and navigation. Before the year was out, however, he had a slight stroke which was followed by a paralysis in one of his legs and an impediment in his speech. He again became an invalid, resting either in his villa at Kamakura or in a hotel at Atami hot springs. Soon he became fairly well but never was active again. When he was living in retirement, he revisited Tosa to see his mother and again in 1875, when he went to see her, he took with him his eldest son, Toichiro. The old woman was happy and proud beyond words to see her grandson, who was a promising medical student at the Tokyo Imperial University. She tried to make their stay as pleasant as possible, serving every day the crisp *sashimi* of sea bream or broiled sea bass or lobsters freshly caught from the Bay of Tosa. While there, Manjiro often took his son fishing and demonstrated his skill by catching several big sea bass every time they went.

The son later studied medicine in Germany and became a successful practitioner, founding several hospitals in Tokyo. When he visited America in 1917, he went to Fairhaven and saw Captain Whitfield's son Marcellus and the people and places associated with his father to express his gratitude in person. Later, in 1918, he presented the town of Fairhaven with a beautiful and historical samurai sword as a token of gratitude.

Long years of recuperation and retirement came to an end at last when Manjiro died quietly of a stroke on November 12, 1898, in his son's house behind Ginza Street, Tokyo. He was buried in the grave which had previously been prepared in the Bussinji Temple, Yanaka, Tokyo.

Thus ended the life of a man who, when a boy, was

shipwrecked and rescued and taken to America as the first Japanese to be educated and live there, who became a voice in the wilderness and patiently taught his countrymen to open their eyes to modern science and Western civilization, who participated in the slow and turbulent development of his country from feudalism to democracy.

Later, in 1925, his remains, together with the tombstone, were moved to the Zoshigaya Cemetery in Tokyo.

In November, 1928, the Japanese Government conferred upon him posthumously the fifth court rank of the senior grade, in appreciation of the unique and invaluable service he had rendered to the nation.

AND AFTER

RECALLING some of his father's anecdotes, Dr. Toichiro Nakahama said on one occasion:

"My father set an example to us children and taught us to be kind to those who were in trouble, to keep promises, to be punctual, to be brave, and to go ahead and do unpleasant things which others hesitated to do. When he was only a lad sailing in the *Franklin*, he jumped into the sea and fought with a ten-foot-long monster turtle when other sailors shrank from such a dangerous feat. He did not back down, and held his own before the captain of a certain ship who acted high-handedly and ordered him about although he lost the chance of sailing in that ship to Japan. Nor was he overawed and frightened into obsequiousness by the Japanese officials who investigated him upon his return to Japan.

"It happened that a certain sailor whom my father used to know lost his job temporarily through no fault of his own and became a vender of refreshments and cakes for the ships staying at the estuary of the Sumida River in Yedo. A local boss demanded the poor sailor pay him a large sum of protection money if he wanted to do business in his territory. As soon as my father learned all about it, he went to see the rogue personally and told him once and for all not to bully the poor sailor. But when the ruffian threatened him with violence, my father actually overpowered him and made him promise to stop blackmailing.

"Furthermore, my father always tried to be kind to the poor and those in trouble. When he was living in the premises of Egawa, there was a deaf-and-dumb beggar who nightly went by, raising a plaintive, inarticulate voice. My father had a few rice balls with red plum pickles in them prepared always for this beggar, and as soon as he heard the quaint voice traveling along the dark street, first faintly and gradually growing louder and louder, he used to go to the gate of his house to give them to the beggar. Whenever he chanced to see a poor sick man lying on the street, he told us children to run along to our house to get medicine or even clothes for him.

"My father used to dine with his family at a restaurant called Kurumaya at Myojinmae, Shiba. On such occasions, if there was any food left on the table when the dinner was over, my father had it packed in a chip box together with the boiled rice and took it away with him to give it to beggars on the street. Needless to say, it was an unthinkable thing in those days for a respectable gentleman to take with him the leftovers of a dinner in a restaurant, no matter for what reason, but my father would never let respectability come between him and charity.

"My father spent an easy and retired life reading English books, visiting his children and friends and dining in first-class restaurants. He often went to see the Kabuki plays at the Shintomiza Theater, which staged the best plays in those days. But to sit on the floor of the theater watching a play, as was the custom of the day, was too much for him, and so he used to order a special chair to sit on in the theater. On the stage of the Shintomiza, once, he saw his own adventure enacted by Sadanji, the greatest actor of the day, but as it proved to be not only untrue but cheap and farcical, he was greatly disappointed.

"Never was my father seen, whenever he went out, without wearing a *hakama* and *haori* with the five crests of our family on it, after the formal Japanese style. Even on a hot summer day, he never failed to be seen without a fine silk gauze *haori*, so that *rikishamen* used to call him 'gentleman in a *haori* with the family crests.' Added to this strictly formal dress, my father used to wear a derby hat and a pair of foreign shoes, a quaint but fashionable style adopted by gentlemen of those days."

On behalf of Dr. Toichiro Nakahama, the eldest son of Manjiro, Viscount Ishii, the Japanese Ambassador to Washington, presented Fairhaven, Massachusetts, with a historical samurai sword on July 4, 1918, in token of the son's gratitude for the kindness shown to his father by the town.

It was a gala occasion with American and Japanese flags and bunting to be seen on every hand in New Bedford and Fairhaven. Soon after nine o'clock in the morning Viscount Ambassador Ishii and his party arrived from Mattapoisett, where they were the house guests of the Honorable Mr. Hamlin. The party went to the New Bedford High School, where exercises were held. Addresses were given by Mayor

Ashley, Lieutenant Governor Coolidge, Viscount Ishii and Mr. Hamlin.

When the exercises in New Bedford were over, the Ambassador and his party were met by a committee from Fairhaven and proceeded to Riverside Cemetery, accompanied by members of the Whitfield family. Ambassador Ishii placed a wreath on the grave of Captain Whitfield, while a simple but impressive ceremony took place. Then the party called at the home of Mrs. Akin, who was then eighty years old, where Manjiro had spent his first two weeks in Fairhaven.

After attending a buffet luncheon, which was held at the Tabitha Inn, the party visited the Memorial Church, the Millicent Library, and the town hall, where the log book of the *John Howland* was shown the guests.

In the meantime, the parade, consisting of a battalion of regulars from Fort Rodman, Naval Reserves, the State Guard from Fairhaven, and the Naval Reserve Band from Newport, was formed on Center Street and proceeded through the important streets of the town to the stadium. After the speakers and guests had ascended to the platform, the men in uniform marched into the stadium. Close behind the speakers' stand was a chorus of school children dressed in white. It is estimated that over ten thousand people witnessed the ceremonies.

After Lieutenant Governor Calvin Coolidge made a welcome address on behalf of the Commonwealth of Massachusetts, Ambassador Ishii said, as he presented the samurai sword:

"This gift may have little intrinsic value, but therein, perhaps, you will find its real value. You are asked to receive it as the concrete token of that something which is without price and above all other values. It is tendered to you at a time in the affairs of a troubled world when men are asking if the old-time virtues of gratitude and honor still hold their places in the human heart. It comes at a time when America and Japan stand linked and resolute in defense of a cause which is so holy — so just and right — that all other considerations vanish to nothingness.

"In this spirit I beg of you, Mr. Chairman, to accept for the town of Fairhaven this tribute of gratitude. The donor would say to the descendants of those who were kind to his revered father that which the whole Japanese people would say to the people of America: — We trust you — we love you, and, if you will let us, we will walk at your side in loyal good fellowship down all the coming years . . ."

At that time, as Japan was fighting World War I shoulder to shoulder with America, particularly cordial relations existed between the two nations. President Woodrow Wilson regretted very much not being able to attend the presentation ceremony because he had to deliver his Fourth of July speech at Mt. Vernon on that day. A few days later, however, he wrote to Ambassador Ishii congratulating him upon the occasion in the following manner:

The White House
    Washington
My Dear Mr. Ambassador:
    May I not give myself the pleasure of saying how much I have been interested in reading your addresses at Fairhaven, Massachusetts, and how grateful I am that the people of that region should have an opportunity of showing you their genuine cordial feeling for yourself and for the great country you represent? The story of Manjiro Nakahama has particularly inter-

ested me. Such links between Japan and America are delightful to remember.

Cordially and sincerely yours,
WOODROW WILSON

Viscount Kikujiro Ishii,
Ambassador of Japan,
Washington, D.C.

Later the late President Franklin Delano Roosevelt wrote to Dr. Nakahama, the eldest son of Manjiro:

The White House
    Washington   June 8, 1933.
My dear Dr. Nakahama:—

When Viscount Ishii was here in Washington he told me that you are living in Tokyo and we talked about your distinguished father.

You may not know that I am the grandson of Mr. Warren Delano of Fairhaven, who was part owner of the ship of Captain Whitfield which brought your father to Fairhaven. Your father lived, as I remembered it, at the house of Mr. Trippe, which was directly across the street from my grandfather's house, and when I was a boy, I well remember my grandfather telling me all about the little Japanese boy who went to school in Fairhaven and who went to church from time to time with the Delano family. I myself used to visit Fairhaven, and my mother's family still own the old house.

The name of Nakahama will always be remembered by my family, and I hope that if you or any of your family come to the United States that you will come to see us.

Believe me, my dear Dr. Nakahama,
Very sincerely yours,
FRANKLIN ROOSEVELT

Dr. Toichiro Nakahama,
Tokyo,
Japan.

More than a century has passed since Manjiro Nakahama lived his life of extraordinary adventure and worked for the rebirth of his country. The spirit of learning which he upheld so courageously, the virtues of kindness and gratitude and humility which were so naturally a part of him, and the international goodwill he embodied in his whole career, have survived the turbulent passage of time.

Manjiro and Captain Whitfield came from opposite ends of the earth, spoke different languages, professed different religions but sailed the same seas, thrilled at the same stars, and shared many deep things.

From a wilderness, Manjiro raised a voice that will echo and re-echo down the years.